Sunshine

Klasse 3/4

Leistungsermittlung 1/2

Cornelsen

Inhaltsverzeichnis

Vorwort 3

Beobachtungsbogen Sprechen Band 1 und 2 4

Kontrollaufgaben Band 1

Unit 1 Meeting friends 8

Unit 2 Pets in the garden 12

Unit 3 At school 18

Unit 4 The second-hand shop 24

Unit 5 Free-time activities 30

Unit 6 In the park 36

Kontrollaufgaben Band 2

Unit 1 A trip to London 42

Unit 2 All year round 48

Unit 3 At the museum 54

Unit 4 Keeping fit 60

Unit 5 Emails from the USA 66

Symbole

 listen to the CD
track 29

 read

 write

Vorwort

Die Diagnose und Dokumentation der Leistungen von Schülerinnen und Schülern im Lernprozess spielt eine wichtige Rolle im Englischunterricht der Grundschule. Das Hauptaugenmerk des Leistungsermittlungsheftes zu *Sunshine* liegt daher auf der systematischen und kontinuierlichen Beobachtung und Erfassung der Lernergebnisse der Kinder. Das Heft bietet Lehrkräften Materialien zur Evaluation der individuellen Lernstände und Lernfortschritte und unterstützt sie bei der Begleitung der Kinder in ihrem Lernprozess. Gleichzeitig stellen die angebotenen Analyseinstrumente eine wichtige Hilfe bei der Ermittlung des konkreten Förderbedarfs dar. Insgesamt kann so ein sinnvoller Beitrag zum lernerfolgsorientierten Unterricht geleistet werden. Das Leistungsermittlungsheft zu *Sunshine* enthält eine Auswahl an Kopiervorlagen, die Lehrkräften Ideen und Hilfen zur Überprüfung der verschiedenen Fertigkeiten bieten:
– Kontrollaufgaben: zahlreiche Aufgaben zur Überprüfung von Fertigkeiten in den Bereichen Hörverstehen, Lesen und Schreiben
– Beobachtungsbogen: ausgewählte Kontexte zur Überprüfung der Sprechfertigkeit

Kontrollaufgaben
Die Kontrollaufgaben beziehen sich auf die einzelnen Units von *Sunshine* und werden von den Kindern selbstständig bearbeitet. Sie decken die Bereiche Hörverstehen, Lesen und Schreiben ab, wobei das Schriftbild im Laufe der Zeit zunehmend an Bedeutung gewinnt.
Mithilfe der Kontrollaufgaben kann die Lehrkraft Rückschlüsse auf Art und Umfang des Erwerbs dieser Fertigkeiten ziehen. Die Aufgaben stellen damit ein Mittel zur Feststellung des bisher Erworbenen dar. So erfährt die Lehrkraft, inwieweit es den Kindern möglich ist, selbstständig mit der im Unterricht gelernten Sprache umzugehen und diese anzuwenden. Die Aufgabentypen sind an Übungen und Materialien aus dem Lehrwerk angelehnt, die den Kindern bereits aus dem Unterricht vertraut sind. Die Hörtexte für die Durchführung der Hörverstehensaufgaben sind auf der beiliegenden CD enthalten.

Um den Kindern das Einhören in den Text und die Kontrolle des Erarbeiteten zu ermöglichen, ist es sinnvoll, die Hörtexte mehrfach abzuspielen. Den Kopiervorlagen mit den Kontrollaufgaben wird jeweils eine Seite mit Anmerkungen für die Lehrkraft gegenübergestellt. Hier finden sich Erläuterungen für den Umgang mit den einzelnen Aufgaben sowie die Hörtexte für die Hörverstehensaufgaben. Auf diese Weise wird eine gute Übersichtlichkeit gewährleistet.

Beobachtungsbogen
Die im Leistungsermittlungsheft enthaltenen Beobachtungsbogen dienen der Überprüfung der Sprechfertigkeit der Kinder/Lernenden. Sie stellen eine sinnvolle Ergänzung zu den in den Hand-reichungen angebotenen Kopiervorlagen zur Beobachtung und Einschätzung von Unterrichtsaktivitäten dar. In den Beobachtungsbogen werden verschiedene Situationen aus dem Lehrwerk vorgeschlagen, die sich besonders für die Über-prüfung von Kompetenzen im Bereich des Sprechens eignen. Dadurch können sowohl individuelle Lernstände ermittelt als auch Lernfortschritte dokumentiert werden.

Der Einsatz der verschiedenen Materialien des Leistungsermittlungsheftes zu *Sunshine* ermöglicht es der Lehrkraft, sich ein differenziertes Bild von den fremdsprachlichen Fähigkeiten der Kinder zu machen. Dabei bietet sich auch eine Vernetzung mit dem in den Handreichungen angebotenen Bogen zur Einschätzung der Lernentwicklung an. Durch die Dokumentation der jeweiligen Lernprozesse werden individuelle Lernfortschritte erkannt und können entsprechend gewürdigt werden. Dadurch kann die Entwicklung einer positiven Einstellung gegenüber der Fremdsprache gefördert und das Vertrauen der Kinder in die eigene Lern- und Leistungsfähigkeit gestärkt werden. Auf diese Weise wird auch ein Beitrag zur Bildung eines tragfähigen Fundaments geleistet, das den Kindern ein motiviertes und erfolgreiches Englischlernen in den weiterführenden Schulen ermöglicht.

Beobachtungsbogen Sprechen

Die vorgeschlagenen Situationen zum Sprechen sind besonders geeignet, die Sprechfertigkeit der Schülerinnen und Schüler zu überprüfen. Zur Leistungsmessung im Bereich Sprechen eignet sich darüber hinaus insbesondere die Stationenarbeit in Stunde 8. Selbstverständlich können Sie auch selbst weitere Situationen zur Leistungsermittlung auswählen.
Kennzeichnung der Leistungen: **++** **+** **−**

Band 1

Name / Sprechsituationen
Unit 1
5.1 Dialogue: Favourite colours
6.2 A colour dictation
8.4 What I can do
Unit 2
2.3 Dialogue: A phone call
4.5 Game: Food for the pets
8.4 What I can do
Unit 3
1.5 What's in your school bag?
4.4 Jack's bad day
6.3 Game: Take five

Band 1

Name																														
Sprechsituationen																														
Unit 4																														
4.3 Dialogue: Clothes																														
5.4 Game: I'm cold																														
7.3 Can I have the gloves, please?																														
Unit 5																														
3.3 About me: Class survey																														
4.2 Portfolio: My favourite activities																														
5.3 Dialogue: Free-time activities																														
6.5 Rooms																														
Unit 6																														
3.5 Game: I'm hungry																														
4.3 How much is an ice cream?																														
5.4 Dialogue: Can I help you?																														
7.3 Portfolio: My favourite ice cream																														

Band 2

Name / Sprechsituationen
Unit 1
4.4 Game: Go to Big Ben
5.2 Dialogue: Buying tickets
7.4 Look at my postcard
Unit 2
4.1 Dialogue: What's the weather like?
4.3 The weather report on TV
6.3 Portfolio: My birthday month
Unit 3
3.4 Dialogue: Where are the animals?
4.3 Talking about animals
6.3 Presentation

Band 2

Sprechsituationen	Name																											
Unit 4																												
5.2 Game: Identity switch																												
5.4 Dialogue: Sport																												
6.3 Presentation																												
Unit 5																												
2.3 Game: When the music stops																												
4.3 About me: Jobs in my family																												
7.2 Acting out the story																												
7.5 What's your name?																												

1 Meeting friends

1 That's English! Hörverstehen

Voraussetzungen
englische Wörter im Alltag;
Chant: That's English!

Spielen Sie den *chant* vor. S nummerieren die Abbildungen in der Reihenfolge, in der die entsprechenden Wörter im *chant* vorkommen.
Der CD-Text wird erneut abgespielt.
S können falls notwendig Fehler korrigieren.

CD track 2
Cowboy, mountain bike, and shop.
That's English!
Popcorn, in-line skates, and stop.
That's English!
Scooter, skateboard, king of pop.
That's English!

2 What's the right number? Hörverstehen

Voraussetzungen
Zahlen 1–10

Spielen Sie den Hörtext von der CD.
S verbinden die Fahrräder mit den passenden Schlössern. Bei den letzten beiden Schlössern tragen sie die gehörten Zahlen ein.
Zur Kontrolle wird der CD-Text erneut abgespielt.

CD track 3
Number 1: The number is 8517.
Number 2: The number is 2639.
Number 3: The number is 2549.
Number 4: The number is 8256.
Number 5: The number is 7135.
Number 6: The number is 6248.

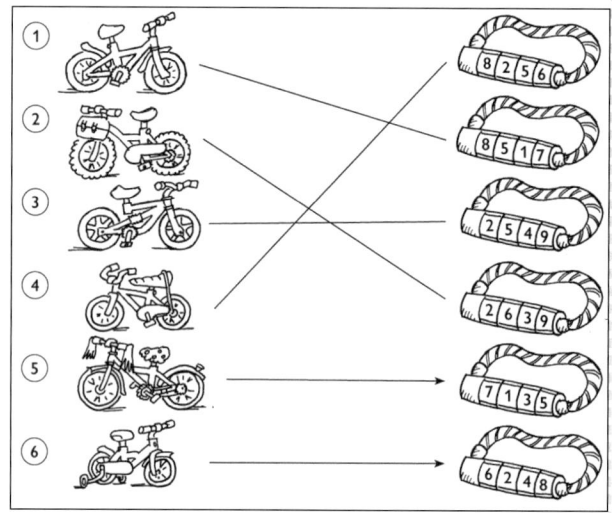

Name Date

1 That's English! Listen. Number the pictures.

track 2

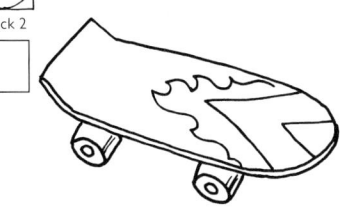

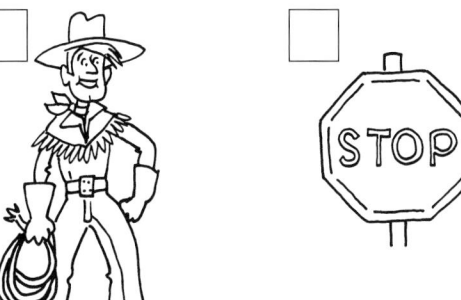

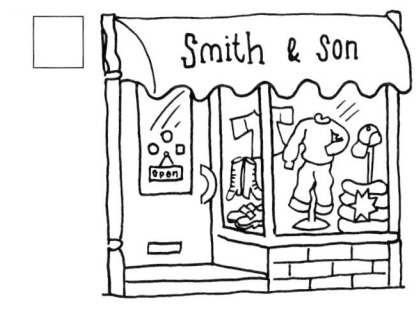

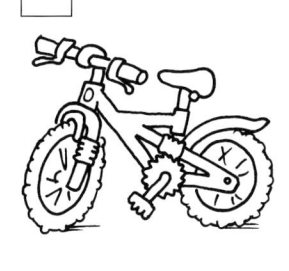

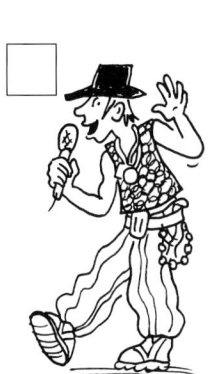

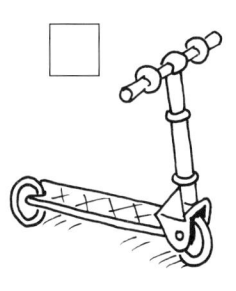

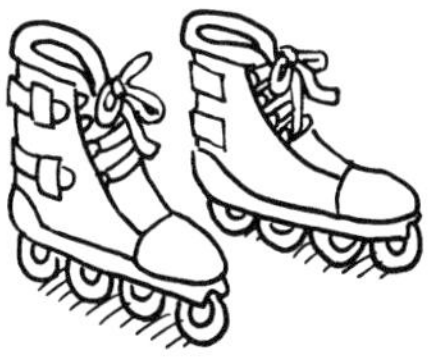

Name Date

2 What's the right number? Listen. Draw lines. Write the missing numbers.

track 3

1

2

3

4

5

6

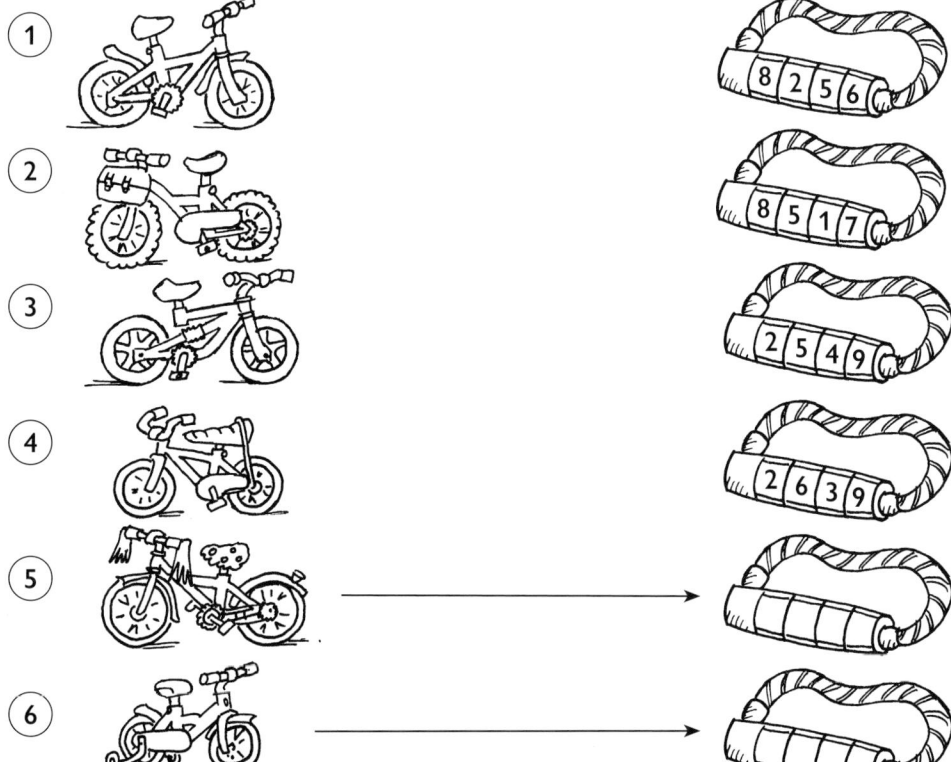

1 Meeting friends

3 What are they saying? Hörverstehen

Voraussetzungen
Begrüßung, Freunde, Spielsachen

S hören den CD-Text und betrachten die Bilder. Beim erneuten Hören ordnen sie die Sätze den entsprechenden Abbildungen zu und nummerieren diese.
Ein letztes Hören dient der Kontrolle.

CD track 4
Number 1: Good morning.
Number 2: What's your name?
Number 3: I've got a skateboard. It's great.
Number 4: Hello, Emma. Come in, please.
Number 5: I'm eight.
Number 6: What's your favourite colour?
Number 7: What's your phone number?
Number 8: I'm not so well.

4 Colours Leseverstehen; Schreiben

Voraussetzungen
Schriftbild: Farben

S lesen die Farbvorschläge und haken ab, in welcher Farbe sie die abgebildeten Gegenstände anschließend ausmalen.
Im zweiten Teil der Aufgabe füllen S die Kästen mit den Lieblingsfarben der Lehrwerkskinder. Anschließend schreiben S ihre Lieblingsfarben auf und malen die Felder entsprechend aus.

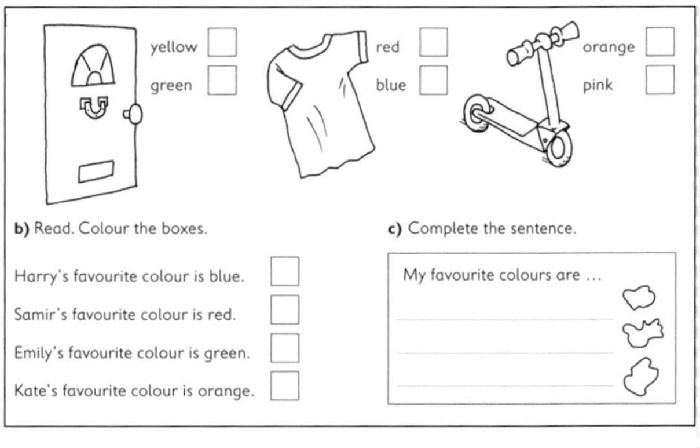

Meeting friends 1

Name _____   Date _____

3 What are they saying? Listen. Number the pictures.

6348177

Bill.

1

Name _____   Date _____

4 Colours a) Choose a colour. Tick the word. Colour the picture.

yellow ☐   red ☐   orange ☐
green ☐   blue ☐   pink ☐

b) Read. Colour the boxes.

Harry's favourite colour is blue. ☐
Samir's favourite colour is red. ☐
Emily's favourite colour is green. ☐
Kate's favourite colour is orange. ☐

c) Complete the sentence.

My favourite colours are …

_____
_____
_____

11

2 Pets in the garden

1 There's a white T-shirt Hörverstehen

Voraussetzungen
Farben

Spielen Sie den Hörtext von der CD.
S malen zunächst die Kreise in den Farben aus,
die in den Aussagen genannt werden.
Dann hören sie den CD-Text erneut und malen die
Bilder in den entsprechenden Farben aus.

CD track 5
I like black cats.
The guinea pig is brown.
There's a white T-shirt.
The carrot is orange.
Emma's house is grey.
Here's my yellow bike.

2 I've got a pet Hörverstehen

Voraussetzungen
Haustiere

S erkennen die Tiernamen in den Aussagen auf der
CD. Sie verbinden die Abbildungen der Kinder mit
den Haustieren, die ihnen gehören.

CD track 6
Tom: Hi, I'm Tom. I've got a hamster.
Boy: The cat is Kitty's pet.
Girl: Have you got a pet, Ted?
Ted: Yes, I have. I've got a guinea pig.
         It's black and white.
Mother: Sandra, please feed your dog.
Father: Where's your rat, Timmy?
Timmy: My rat? It's in the garden shed.

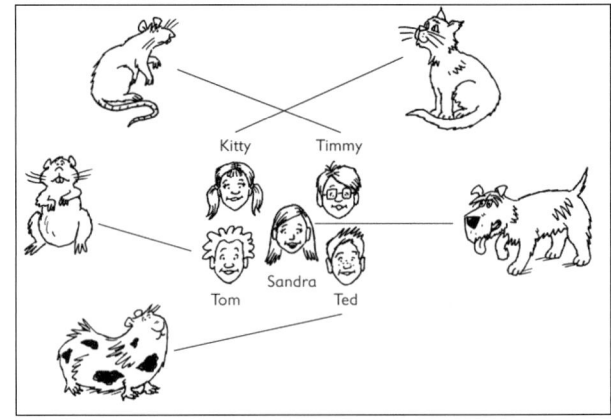

Pets in the garden 2

Name _____ Date _____

1 There's a white T-shirt Listen. Colour the circles. Colour the pictures.

track 5

Name _____ Date _____

2 I've got a pet Listen. Draw lines from the children to their pets.

track 6

Kitty   Timmy

Tom   Sandra   Ted

2 Pets in the garden

3 Food for the pets Hörverstehen

Voraussetzungen
Haustiere, Lebensmittel

S hören die Dialoge von der CD.
Sie verbinden die Tiere mit den Lebensmitteln.
Außerdem werden die positiven Aussagen mit
„Smileys", die negativen mit „Frowneys"
gekennzeichnet.
Das wiederholte Hören dient der Kontrolle.

CD track 7
Girl: My hamster is hungry.
Boy: Here's some lettuce.
Girl: Thank you.

Boy: My cat is hungry.
Girl: Here's some bread.
Boy: Bread for my cat? No, thank you.

Girl: My rabbit is hungry.
Man: Here are some carrots.
Girl: My rabbit likes carrots. Thank you.

Woman: Here are some peanuts for your hungry guinea pig.
Boy: Thank you. My guinea pig likes peanuts.
Girl: My dog is hungry.
Boy: I've got some apples for your dog.
Girl: Apples? No, thank you.

4 I like carrots Hörverstehen; Leseverstehen

Voraussetzungen
Vorlieben und Abneigungen;
Schriftbild: Haustiere, Lebensmittel

S hören die Aussagen von der CD.
Sie erkennen die positiven und die negativen
Aussagen, ordnen sie den passenden Abbildungen
und Wörtern zu und kennzeichnen
diese entsprechend.
Ein weiteres Hören dient der Kontrolle.

CD track 8
Number 1
I like my friend Jim.
I like carrots.
I don't like lettuce.
I like the colour white.
I like my rabbit.
I don't like the colour black.
I like Sue's garden shed.
I like parties.

Number 2
I don't like the colour green.
I like green apples.
I like my guinea pig.
I don't like rats.
I like cats.

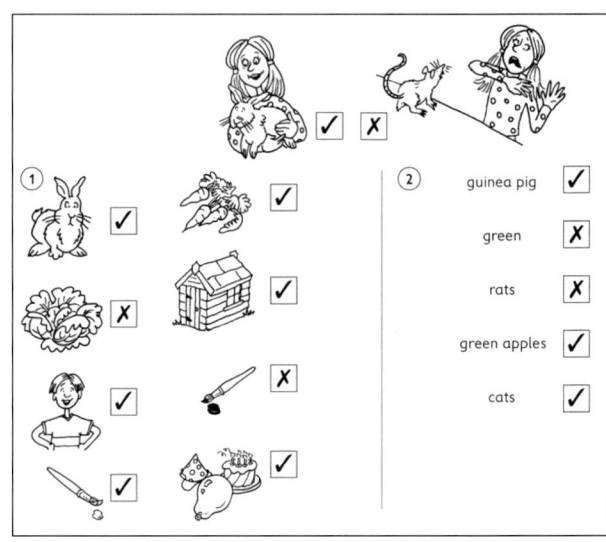

Pets in the garden 2

Name _____   Date _____

3 Food for the pets Listen. Draw lines. Draw the faces: 😊 ☹.

track 7

Name _____   Date _____

4 I like carrots Listen. What do the children like? Tick or cross out.

track 8

①

②
guinea pig ☐

green ☐

rats ☐

green apples ☐

cats ☐

15

2 Pets in the garden

5 Come to my party Leseverstehen

Voraussetzungen
Schriftbild: Haustiere, Lebensmittel;
Story: Rabbit's party

S lesen die Sätze und nummerieren sie, sodass sie einen sinnvollen Dialog ergeben. Anschließend verbinden sie die Aussagen mit den dazu passenden Abbildungen.

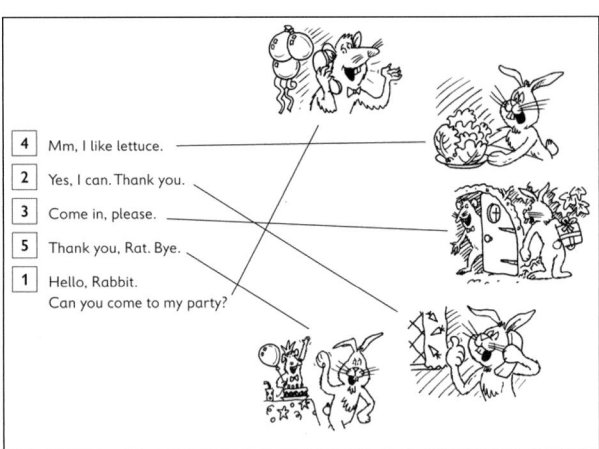

6 Food – colours – pets Leseverstehen; Schreiben

Voraussetzungen
Schriftbild: Farben, Haustiere, Lebensmittel

S lesen die Wörter. Sie kreisen sie den Wortfeldern entsprechend in den angegebenen Farben ein und schreiben sie in die richtigen Spalten.
Die Wörter, die übrig bleiben, werden durchgestrichen.

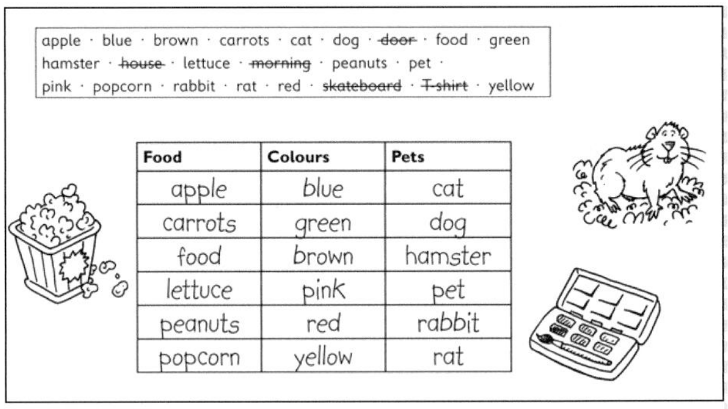

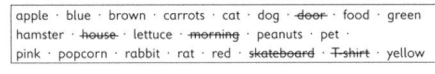

Food	Colours	Pets
apple	blue	cat
carrots	green	dog
food	brown	hamster
lettuce	pink	pet
peanuts	red	rabbit
popcorn	yellow	rat

Pets in the garden 2

Name _____ Date _____

5 Come to my party Read and number the sentences. Draw lines.

☐ Mm, I like lettuce.

☐ Yes, I can. Thank you.

☐ Come in, please.

☐ Thank you, Rat. Bye.

☐ Hello, Rabbit.
  Can you come to my party?

Name _____ Date _____

6 Food – colours – pets

a) Circle the words: food = yellow; colours = green; pets = brown.
   Which words don't fit? Cross them out.

apple · blue · brown · carrots · cat · dog · door · food · green hamster · house · lettuce · morning · peanuts · pet · pink · popcorn · rabbit · rat · red · skateboard · T-shirt · yellow

b) Write the words.

Food	Colours	Pets
apple	blue	cat

3 At school

1 There's the school bus Hörverstehen

Voraussetzungen
Lebensmittel, Schule, Schulgegenstände

Spielen Sie den Hörtext von der CD.
S ordnen die Hörabschnitte den richtigen Abbildungen zu und nummerieren diese entsprechend.
Ein abschließendes Hören dient der Kontrolle.

CD track 9
Number 1
Father: There's the school bus. Hurry, Ann.
Ann: Yes, Dad. Bye.

Number 2
Boy: There's my school. I like my school.

Number 3
Teacher: Take your rubber, your pencil and your ruler. Oh – no. What's that in your school bag?
Girl: Sorry – that's my rat.

Number 4
Girl: Mrs Jones, Tom has got my pencil case.
Tom: No, I haven't.
Girl: Yes, you have.
Tom: No, I haven't. But I've got your book.

Number 5
Boy: What's in my lunch box, Mum?
Mother: Two carrots and some peanuts.

Number 6
Girl: I don't like carrots. But I like peanuts.
Boy: Have you got peanuts in your lunch box?
Girl: No, I haven't. I've got a sandwich and an apple in my lunch box.

2 What's in your pencil case? Hörverstehen

Voraussetzungen
Zahlen 1–10, Schulgegenstände

Spielen Sie die Dialoge von der CD.
S notieren die Anzahl der Schulgegenstände in den Federmappen der Kinder.
Ein weiteres Hören dient der Kontrolle.

CD track 10
Teacher: Let's check your pencil cases. Tim, have you got pencils in your pencil case?
Tim: Yes, I have. I've got three pencils.
Teacher: Good. Have you got a pen?
Tim: Yes, here's my pen.
Teacher: What else have you got?
Tim: I've got a ruler and five felt tips. Sorry, I haven't got a rubber.

Teacher: Ann, what have you got in your pencil case?
Ann: I've got a pen and a ruler in my pencil case.
Teacher: Have you got felt tips?
Ann: Yes, I have. I've got eight felt tips and I've got four pencils.
Teacher: Good, Ann. Have you got scissors?
Ann: I haven't got scissors, sorry.

Teacher: What about you, Bill? Have you got a rubber?
Bill: Yes, I have. I've got two rubbers.
Teacher: Have you got scissors?
Bill: Here are my scissors.
Teacher: Have you got a glue stick?
Bill: Oops – I haven't got a glue stick.
Teacher: What else is in your pencil case?
Bill: I've got two pencils and a pencil sharpener.

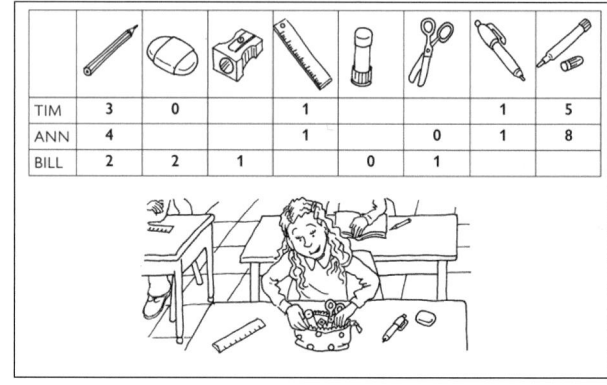

At school 3

Name _____ Date _____

1 There's the school bus Listen. Number the pictures.

track 9

Name _____ Date _____

2 What's in your pencil case? Listen. Write the numbers.

track 10

TIM								
ANN								
BILL								

3 At school

3 School activities Hörverstehen

Voraussetzungen
Schulgegenstände, Aktivitäten in der Schule

S hören die Anordnungen von der CD.
Sie nummerieren zunächst nur die Tätigkeiten.
Spielen Sie den Hörtext ein zweites Mal.
S verbinden die Abbildungen der Tätigkeiten mit den genannten Gegenständen.
Zum Schluss führen S die Anweisungen aus und zeichnen die Gegenstände bzw. schreiben ihren Namen.
Zur Kontrolle wird der CD-Text erneut abgespielt.

CD track 11
Number 1: Take your book and read.
Number 2: Take a pen and write your name.
Number 3: Take a pencil and draw a rubber.
Number 4: Draw an apple. Take a green felt tip and colour the apple green.

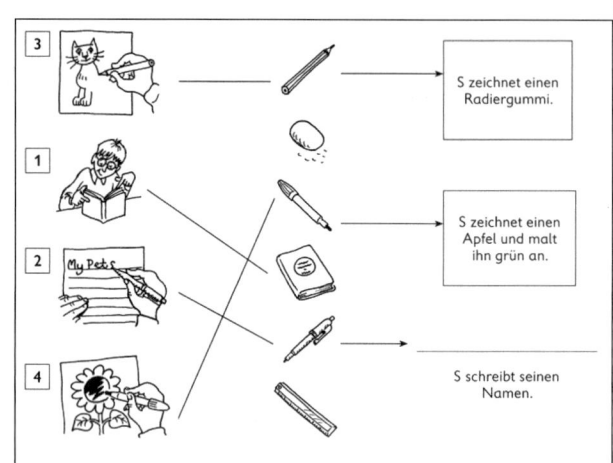

4 That's my rubber Hörverstehen

Voraussetzungen
Schulgegenstände

S hören vier Aussagen bzw. Dialoge, in denen es um einen Radiergummi geht. Sie nummerieren die entsprechenden Abbildungen.

CD track 12
Number 1
Girl: That's my rubber. Give it back.

Number 2
Boy 1: Have you got a rubber?
Boy 2: Sorry, I haven't got a rubber.

Number 3
Boy: Can I have your rubber, please?
Girl: Yes, here you are.

Number 4
Boy: I've got two rubbers in my pencil case.

Name ______________________ Date __________

track 11

3 School activities

Listen. Number the pictures. Draw lines. Do the activities.

☐

☐

☐

☐

 → ☐

 → ☐

 → ______________

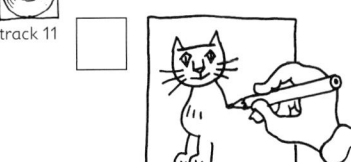

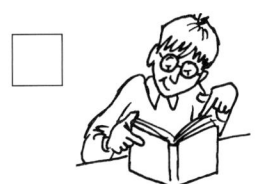

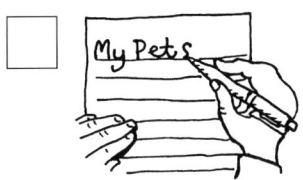

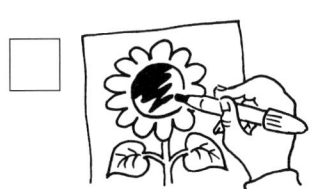

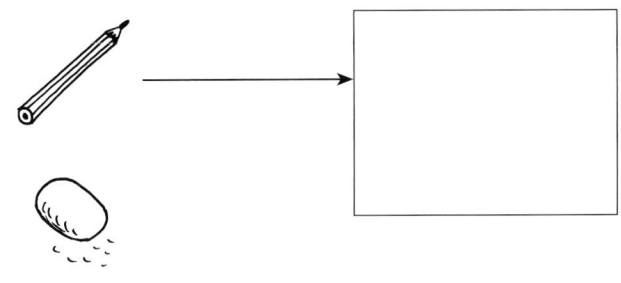

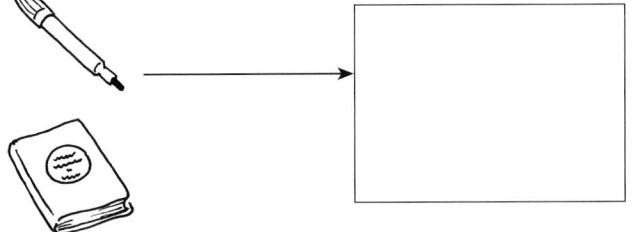

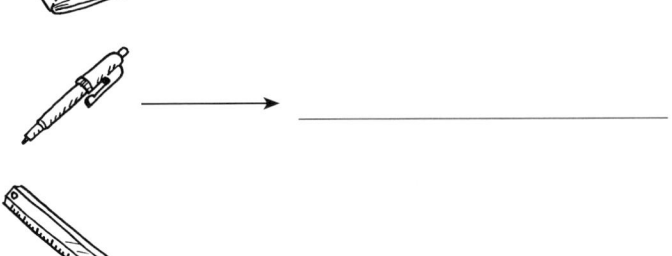

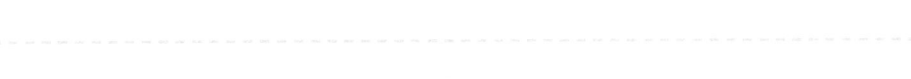

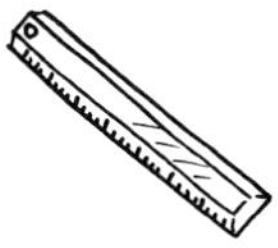

Name ______________________ Date __________

track 12

4 That's my rubber

Listen. Number the pictures.

☐

☐

☐

☐

☐

☐

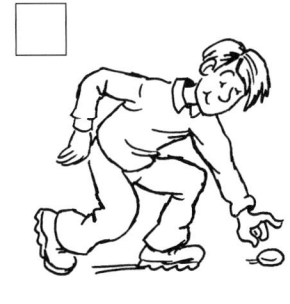

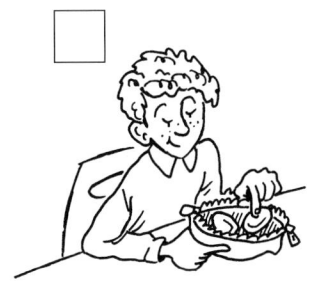

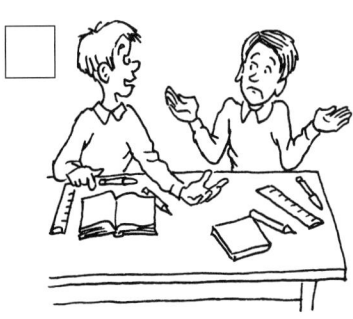

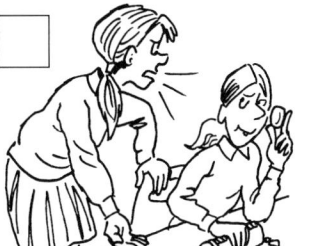

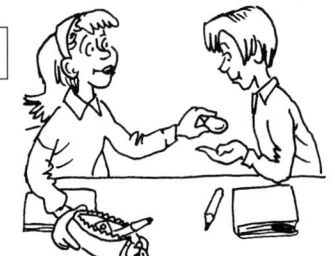

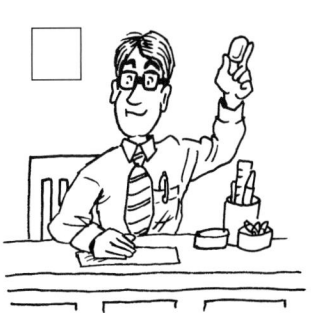

3 At school

5 Read, draw, write and colour Leseverstehen

Voraussetzungen

Schriftbild: Farben, Schulgegenstände, Aktivitäten in der Schule

S können sich im ersten Teil der Aufgabe für jeweils einen der Schulgegenstände bzw. eine der genannten Farben entscheiden. Die nicht zutreffenden Begriffe werden durchgestrichen. Anschließend führen S die jeweiligen Anweisungen aus.
Im zweiten Teil lesen S den Text und zeichnen Toms Lieblingsfarbe in den Kreis. Zusätzlich kann auch das Wort geschrieben werden.

① Draw a school bus/a school bag.
   Colour it orange/red.

② Draw a yellow pencil case/a pink lunch box.
   Write your name on it.

I'm Tom.
I've got a blue school bag. Ben's school bag is green and yellow.
My lunch box is blue and I've got a blue bike.
I don't like pink.
Ann's skateboard is pink. I've got a blue skateboard.
My favourite colour is ___blue___ ◯

6 At school Leseverstehen; Schreiben

Voraussetzungen

Schriftbild: Schulgegenstände, Aktivitäten in der Schule

S lesen die Wörter im Kasten. Sie ergänzen die fehlenden Wörter im Lückentext und orientieren sich dabei an den Abbildungen. Sie kreisen die verwendeten Begriffe aus dem Kasten ein.

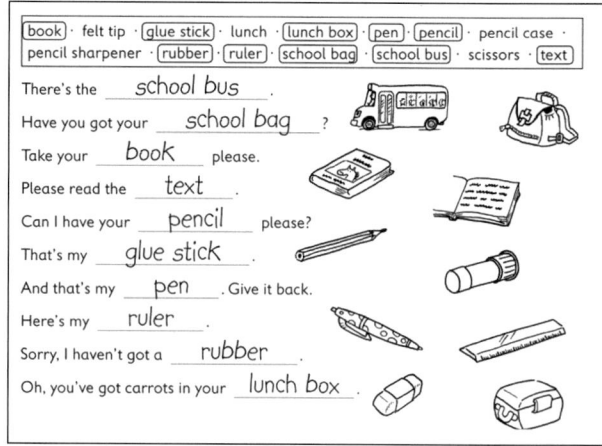

book · felt tip · (glue stick) · lunch · (lunch box) · (pen) · (pencil) · pencil case
pencil sharpener · (rubber) · (ruler) · (school bag) · (school bus) · scissors · (text)

There's the ___school bus___ .
Have you got your ___school bag___ ?
Take your ___book___ please.
Please read the ___text___ .
Can I have your ___pencil___ please?
That's my ___glue stick___ .
And that's my ___pen___ . Give it back.
Here's my ___ruler___ .
Sorry, I haven't got a ___rubber___ .
Oh, you've got carrots in your ___lunch box___ .

At school 3

Name _____ Date _____

5 Read, draw, write and colour

a) Read the sentences. Choose a word. Do the activity.

① Draw a school bus/a school bag.
   Colour it orange/red.

② Draw a yellow pencil case/a pink lunch box.
   Write your name on it.

b) Read the text. Colour the circle.
Write the missing word.

I'm Tom.
I've got a blue school bag. Ben's school bag is green and yellow.
My lunch box is blue and I've got a blue bike.
I don't like pink.
Ann's skateboard is pink. I've got a blue skateboard.
My favourite colour is _____ ◯

Name _____ Date _____

6 At school Read the words in the box. Write the missing words. Circle them in the box.

book · felt tip · glue stick · lunch · lunch box · pen · pencil · pencil case · pencil sharpener · rubber · ruler · school bag · school bus · scissors · text

There's the _____ .

Have you got your _____ ?

Take your _____ please.

Please read the _____ .

Can I have your _____ please?

That's my _____ .

And that's my _____ . Give it back.

Here's my _____ .

Sorry, I haven't got a _____ .

Oh, you've got carrots in your _____ .

4 The second-hand shop

1 Clothes Hörverstehen

Voraussetzungen
Kleidung

S sehen sich die Kleidungsstücke an.
Sie hören den CD-Text und verbinden
die Abbildungen der Kleidungsstücke
mit den Schränken der genannten Kinder.

CD track 13
Kitty has got a skirt, a jacket and a dress.
Bob has got a shirt, trousers and a pullover.
Sue has got a pullover, jeans and a skirt.
Tim has got a jacket, a pullover and trousers.

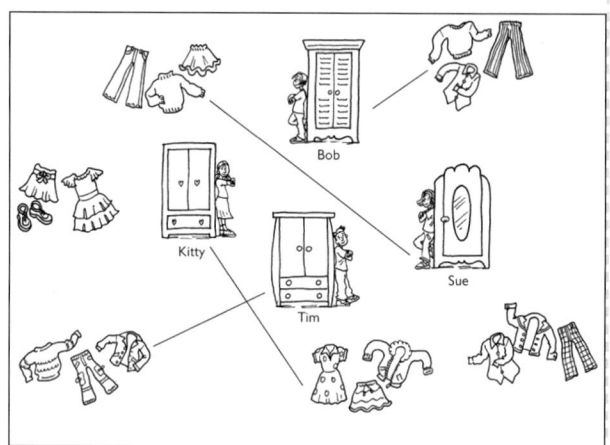

2 Too big or too small? Hörverstehen

Voraussetzungen
Kleidung, Adjektive

S hören den CD-Text.
Sie entscheiden, welche der Aussagen richtig sind
und welche nicht, und markieren die Abbildungen
entsprechend.
Ein wiederholtes Hören dient der Kontrolle.

CD track 14
Anne is wearing a dress. The dress is too big.
This is Sue. She's wearing a jacket. The jacket is too small.
Tom is wearing a shirt. The shirt is too big.
Look at Joe. He's wearing gloves. The gloves are too small.
Helen is wearing a skirt. The skirt is too small.
There's Eric. He's wearing trousers. The trousers are too big.
And Jack? Jack is wearing a hat. The hat is too small.

The second-hand shop 4

Name _____   Date _____

1 Clothes Listen and draw lines.

Bob

Kitty

Tim

Sue

Name _____   Date _____

2 Too big or too small? Listen. Tick or cross out: right ✓ wrong ✗.

Anne ☐   Tom ☐   Eric ☐   Sue ☐

Joe ☐   Jack ☐   Helen ☐

25

4 The second-hand shop

3 Do you like the shoes? Hörverstehen

Voraussetzungen
Kleidung, Bestätigung und Verneinung

Spielen Sie die Dialoge von der CD.
Den Aussagen entsprechend markieren S die passenden Abbildungen mit einem „Smiley" bzw. einem „Frowney".
Ein wiederholtes Hören dient der Kontrolle.

CD track 15
Girl: Do you like the shoes?
Boy: No, I don't.

Girl: Here's a nice dress. Do you like it?
Boy: Yes, I do.

Girl: Mm – a white skirt. Do you like it?
Boy: No, I don't.

Girl: Do you like black jeans?
Boy: Yes, I do.

Girl: Here's my mother's favourite hat. Do you like it?
Boy: Yes, I do.

Girl: I don't like my father's jacket. Do you like it?
Boy: No, I don't.

4 My hands are cold Hörverstehen; Leseverstehen

Voraussetzungen
Körperteile; Schriftbild: Kleidung

S hören die Dialoge von der CD und nummerieren die genannten Körperteile.
Die CD wird erneut abgespielt. S lesen die Wörter und verbinden die Körperteile mit den entsprechenden Kleidungsstücken.
Ein letztes Hören dient der Kontrolle.

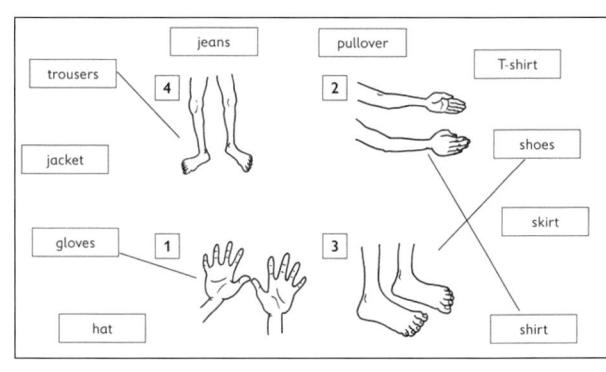

CD track 16
Number 1
Girl 1:   My hands are cold.
Girl 2:   Here are some warm gloves.

Number 2
Boy: My arms are cold.
Mother: I've got a warm shirt for you.

Number 3
Girl: My feet are cold.
Mother: Here are some shoes for you.

Number 4
Boy: My legs are cold.
Mother: I've got some warm trousers for you.

The second-hand shop 4

Name _____ Date _____

3 Do you like the shoes? Listen. Draw the faces: 😊 😊 .

track 15

Name _____ Date _____

4 My hands are cold Listen. Number the pictures. Read the words. Draw lines.

track 16

trousers   jeans   pullover   T-shirt

jacket   shoes

gloves   skirt

hat   shirt

27

4 The second-hand shop

5 I'm wearing a dress Leseverstehen

Voraussetzungen
Schriftbild: Farben, Kleidung, Adjektive

S lesen die Beschreibungen der Kinder und vergleichen sie mit den Abbildungen.
Sie schreiben die Namen der Kinder unter die passenden Bilder und streichen die nicht zutreffenden Wörter im Text durch.
Sie malen die Gegenstände aus, für die eine Farbe angegeben ist.

6 What I'm wearing Leseverstehen; Schreiben

Voraussetzungen
Schriftbild: Farben, Kleidung, Adjektive

S lesen die Wörter im Kasten und schreiben sie in die passenden Textlücken. Die verwendeten Begriffe werden im Kasten durchgestrichen.
S malen die Kleidungsstücke entsprechend den Angaben aus.
Sie zeichnen den Gegenstand, der im Wortkasten übrig geblieben ist, und schreiben die Wörter: *a red dress*.

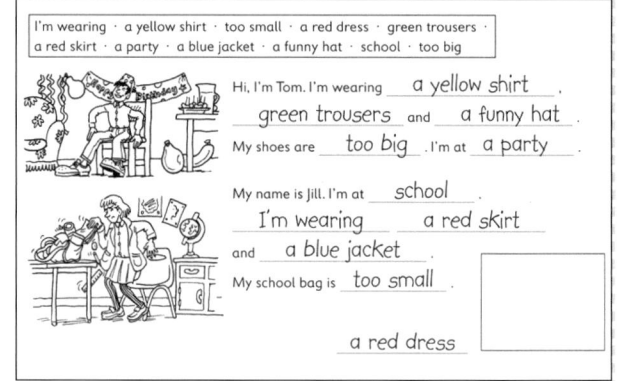

The second-hand shop 4

Name _____   Date _____

5 I'm wearing a dress Read. Write the names. Cross out the wrong words.
Colour the pictures.

My name is Sarah.	I'm Ann.	Hello, my name is Sue.
I'm wearing a T-shirt /	I'm wearing a skirt / a hat.	My pullover / jacket is too
a shirt. It's blue.	It's yellow and orange.	big.
My trousers / shoes are	My shoes / gloves are	I'm warm / cold.
blue.	green.	I'm wearing a hat / gloves.
I've got in-line skates /	I like my guinea pig /	There's my school bag /
a scooter.	rabbit.	bike. It's red.

Name _____   Date _____

6 What I'm wearing a) Read and write the words. Cross them out in the box.
Colour the pictures.

I'm wearing · a yellow shirt · too small · a red dress · green trousers ·
a red skirt · a party · a blue jacket · a funny hat · school · too big

Hi, I'm Tom. I'm wearing _____ ,
_____ and _____ .

My shoes are _____ . I'm at _____ .

My name is Jill. I'm at _____ .
_____ _____
and _____ .

My school bag is _____ .

b) What isn't in the pictures? Write and draw.

29

5 Free-time activities

1 I like reading Hörverstehen

Voraussetzungen
Freizeitaktivitäten, Vorlieben und Abneigungen

S hören die Aussagen von der CD.
Sie verbinden die Kinder mit den Tätigkeiten,
die diese mögen bzw. ablehnen.
Ein letztes Hören dient der Kontrolle.

CD track 17
I'm Emma. I don't like playing
computer games. Meeting friends
and listening to music is great.

Hello, my name is David.
Watching TV is boring. I like
meeting my friends and playing football.

Hi, my name is Ben.
I like reading and watching TV.
Playing football? No, thank you.

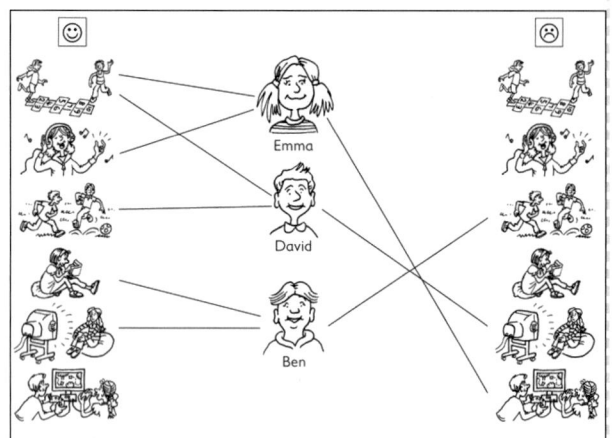

2 A TV in Kate's bedroom Hörverstehen

Voraussetzungen
Räume im Haus

Spielen Sie den Hörtext von der CD.
S sehen sich die abgebildeten Räume an.
Sie überprüfen die Aussagen und haken ab,
ob diese richtig oder falsch sind.

CD track 18
Number 1:   There's a TV in Kate's bedroom.
Number 2:   There's a book in the living room.
Number 3:   There's a school bag in the kitchen.
Number 4:   There's a rat in the bathroom.
Number 5:   There's a cat in the living room.
Number 6:   There's a lunch box in the kitchen.
Number 7:   There's a shoe in the bathroom.
Number 8:   There's a skirt in the bedroom.
Number 9:   There's a lettuce in the kitchen.
Number 10: There's a TV in the living room.
Number 11: There's a pencil case in Kate's bedroom.
Number 12: There's a rabbit in Kate's bedroom.

Free-time activities 5

Name _____ Date _____

1 I like reading Listen. What do the children like? Draw lines.

Emma

David

Ben

Name _____ Date _____

2 A TV in Kate's bedroom Listen and tick.

	right 👍	wrong 👎
1		
2		
3		
4		
5		
6		
7		
8		
9		
10		
11		
12		

5 Free-time activities

3 Where's my school bag? Hörverstehen

Voraussetzungen
Räume im Haus

S hören die Dialoge von der CD.
Sie verbinden die Gegenstände mit den Orten,
an denen diese zu finden sind.
Ein weiteres Hören dient der Kontrolle.

CD track 19
Girl: Mum, where's my school bag? It isn't in my bedroom.
Mother: What about the kitchen?
Girl: Yes, here it is. Thank you.

Father: Where's your rabbit? Is it in the house?
Boy: No, it isn't. It's in the garden shed.

Boy 1: Is the TV in your bedroom?
Boy 2: No, it isn't. It's in the living room.

Mother: Where's the dog, Sam? Is it in the bathroom?
Sam: Yes, Mum, it is.

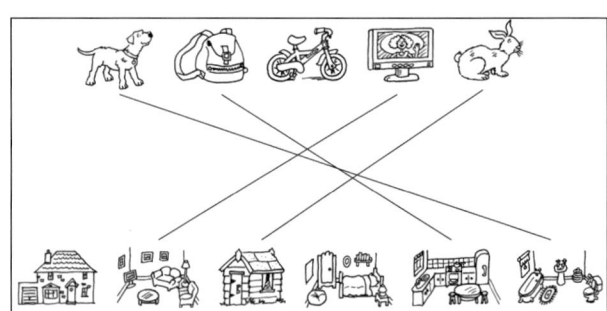

4 Free-time activities Hörverstehen; Leseverstehen

Voraussetzungen
Schriftbild: Freizeitaktivitäten, Vorlieben
und Abneigungen

S hören die Geräusche von der CD und
nummerieren die Abbildungen entsprechend.
Sie lesen die Sätze und verbinden sie mit den
passenden Abbildungen.

CD track 20
Different sounds:
Number 1: Somebody kicking a football.
Number 2: Music playing.
Number 3: Children talking and giggling.
Number 4: Sound of a talk-show on TV.
Number 5: Clattering noises from a keyboard
and sounds from a computer game.
Number 6: Somebody turning the pages of a book.

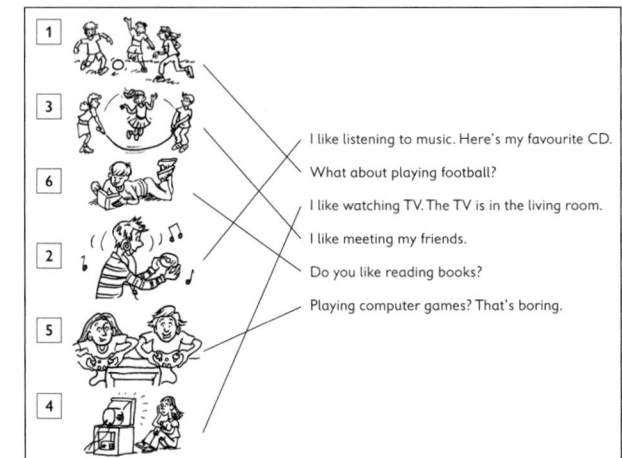

Name ______________________ Date __________

track 19

3 Where's my school bag? Listen. Draw lines.

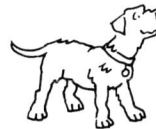

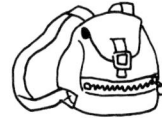

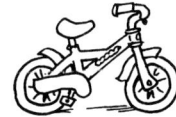

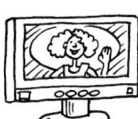

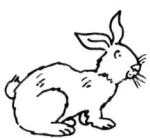

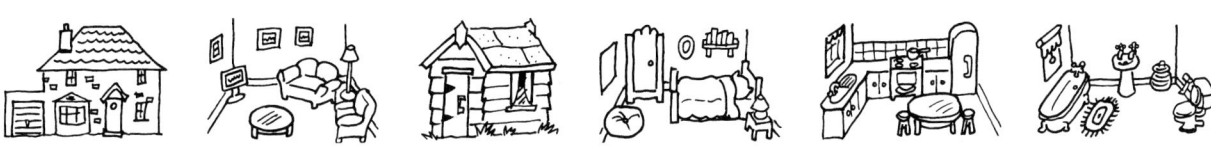

Name ______________________ Date __________

track 20

4 Free-time activities Listen. Number the pictures. Read the sentences. Draw lines.

☐

☐

☐

☐

☐

☐

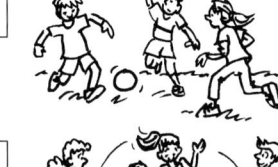

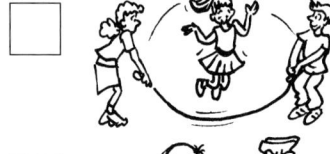

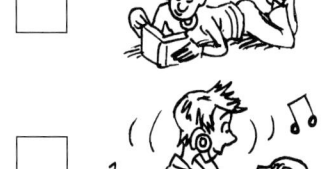

I like listening to music. Here's my favourite CD.

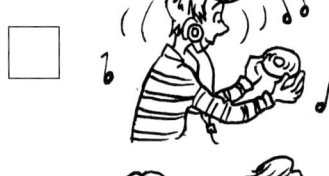

What about playing football?

I like watching TV. The TV is in the living room.

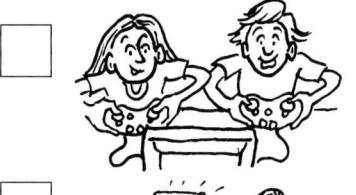

I like meeting my friends.

Do you like reading books?

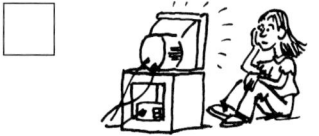

Playing computer games? That's boring.

5 Free-time activities

5 Where's the cat? Leseverstehen

Voraussetzungen
Schriftbild: Räume im Haus;
Reim: Where's the cat?

S lesen die Zeilen des Reims und ziehen Linien zu den jeweils passenden Abbildungen.

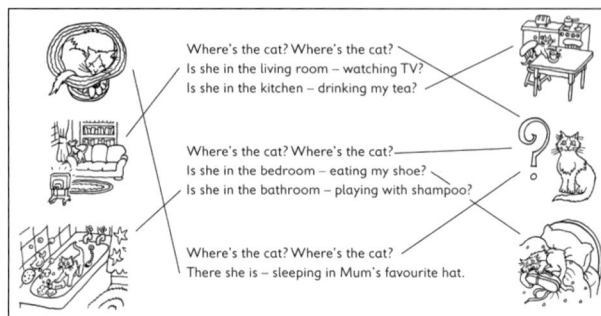

6 Questions and answers Leseverstehen; Schreiben

Voraussetzungen
Schriftbild: Freizeitaktivitäten, Räume im Haus

S lesen die Fragen und schreiben die passenden Antworten aus dem Kasten dazu.
Geben Sie einen Zeitraum vor, in dem S überprüfen, ob sie die Sätze richtig übertragen haben.

What about meeting your friends, Emily? · No, it isn't. It's in my bedroom ·
Great idea. I like that CD. · She's in the kitchen. · No, I don't. It's boring.

1. Where's your cat?
   She's in the kitchen.
2. What about listening to this music?
   Great idea. I like that CD.
3. Do you like the computer game?
   No, I don't. It's boring.
4. Is your skateboard in the garden shed?
   No, it isn't. It's in my bedroom.
5. Watching TV is boring.
   What about meeting your friends, Emily?
   Great idea.

Free-time activities 5

Name _____ Date _____

5 Where's the cat? Read the rhyme. Draw lines to the pictures.

Where's the cat? Where's the cat?
Is she in the living room – watching TV?
Is she in the kitchen – drinking my tea?

Where's the cat? Where's the cat?
Is she in the bedroom – eating my shoe?
Is she in the bathroom – playing with shampoo?

Where's the cat? Where's the cat?
There she is – sleeping in Mum's favourite hat.

Name _____ Date _____

6 Questions and answers Read the questions. Write the answers.

> What about meeting your friends, Emily? · No, it isn't. It's in my bedroom. ·
> Great idea. I like that CD. · She's in the kitchen. · No, I don't. It's boring.

(1) Where's your cat?
_____

(2) What about listening to this music?
_____

(3) Do you like the computer game?
_____

(4) Is your skateboard in the garden shed?
_____

(5) Watching TV is boring.
_____
Great idea.

6 In the park

1 I'm thirsty Hörverstehen

Voraussetzungen
Adjektive

S hören die Aussagen von der CD.
Zu jeder der Aussagen passt eine von drei Abbildungen.
S finden die richtigen Abbildungen und kreisen sie ein.

CD track 21
Number 1:   I'm thirsty.
Number 2:   My guinea pig is hungry.
Number 3:   Wow, it's so hot.
Number 4:   Brr, it's cold today.
Number 5:   I'm hungry.
Number 6:   What's his name?

2 Shopping Hörverstehen

Voraussetzungen
Lebensmittel, Einkauf, Zahlen 20–100

S hören die Verkaufsgespräche von der CD und haken die Waren ab, die gekauft werden.
Ein erneutes Abspielen des Hörtextes dient der Kontrolle.

CD track 22
Boy: Have you got chocolate milk?
Shopkeeper: No, I haven't. But I have vanilla milk. Is that OK?
Boy: Yes, thank you.

Woman: How much is that sandwich?
Shopkeeper: It's 70 p.
Woman: 70 p. Here you are.

Girl: Can I have some juice, please?
Shopkeeper: Orange juice or apple juice?
Girl: Orange juice, please.

Man: I'd like a peach, please.
Shopkeeper: A big peach is 30 p, a small peach is 20 p.
Man: I'd like the small peach, please.

Girl: I'd like a strawberry ice cream, please.
Shopkeeper: Here you are.

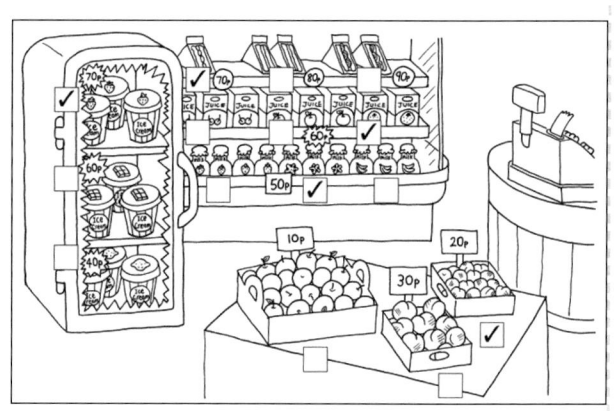

In the park 6

Name _____   Date _____

1 I'm thirsty Listen. Circle the right pictures.

track 21

① ② ③
④ ⑤ ⑥

Name _____   Date _____

2 Shopping Tick the right food.

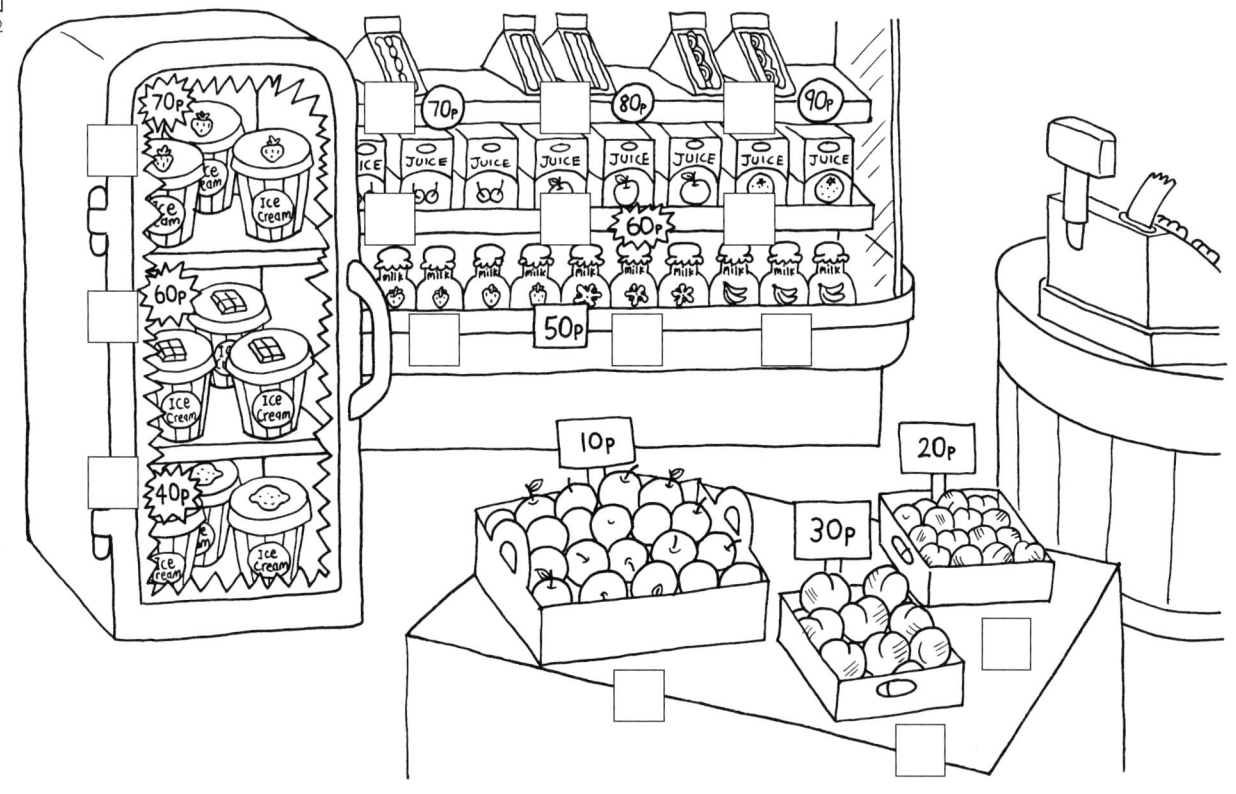

track 22

37

6 In the park

3 I like banana ice cream Hörverstehen

Voraussetzungen
Lebensmittel, Obst, Vorlieben und Abneigungen

Spielen Sie den Hörtext von der CD.
S erfahren, welche Eissorten die Kinder mögen bzw. nicht mögen, und machen entsprechende Eintragungen in die Liste.
Ein abschließendes Hören der CD dient der Kontrolle.

CD track 23
Girl: What are your favourite ice creams, Tom?
Tom: My favourite ice creams are orange
 ice cream and lemon ice cream.
 But I don't like peach ice cream.

Girl: Do you like strawberry ice cream, Sue?
Sue: No, I don't like strawberry ice cream.
 But I like vanilla ice cream and cherry ice cream.

Boy: David, what about some ice cream?
David: Great idea! I like apple ice cream
 and strawberry ice cream.
 No banana ice cream for me – no thank you!

Boy: I'm hot. What about some ice cream, Emma?
Emma: Great idea! Peach ice cream for me.
 And I like chocolate ice cream.
 And, and, … some lemon ice cream, please.

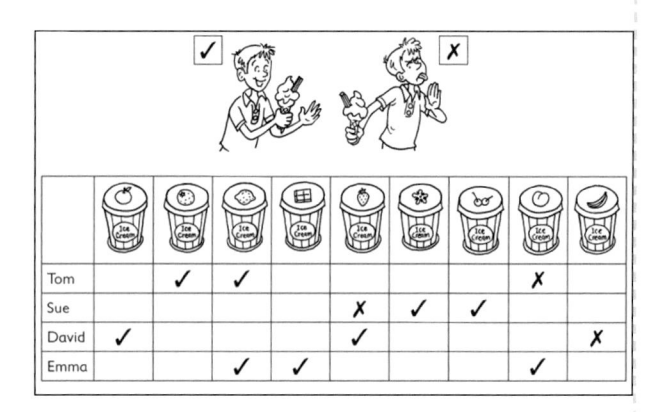

4 How much is the skateboard? Hörverstehen

Voraussetzungen
Einkauf, Zahlen 1–12, 20–100

Spielen Sie den Hörtext von der CD.
S erfahren, wie viel die abgebildeten Gegenstände kosten, und verbinden sie mit den angegebenen Preisen. Ein zweites Hören dient der Kontrolle.

CD track 24
Boy: How much is the skateboard?
Shop-assistant: It's 40 pounds.

Girl: I like the dress. How much is it?
Shop-assistant: It's 30 pounds.

Boy: How much is a banana?
Shopkeeper: One banana is 20 p.
 Three bananas are 50 p.

Woman: That big lettuce – how much is it?
Shopkeeper: It's 80 p.

Girl: How much are the peanuts?
Shopkeeper: They're 30 p.

Boy: I haven't got any rat food.
 How much is it?
Shopkeeper: It's 90 p.

Girl: Wow – I like the mountain bike.
 How much is it?
Shop-assistant: It's 60 pounds.

Boy: How much is a carrot?
Shopkeeper: A carrot is 11 p – sorry – no, it's 7 p.

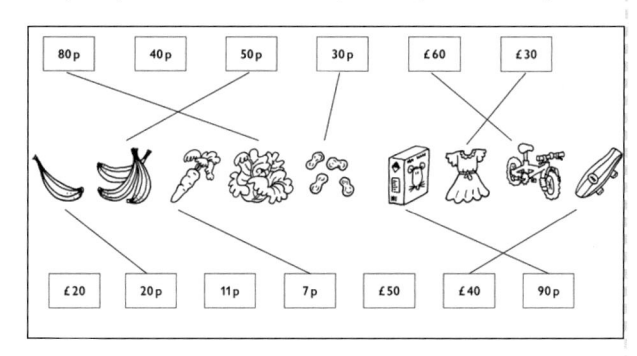

In the park 6

Name _____ Date _____

3 I like banana ice cream Listen. Tick or cross out.

track 23

Tom									
Sue									
David									
Emma									

Name _____ Date _____

4 How much is the skateboard? Listen. Draw lines.

track 24

| 80 p | 40 p | 50 p | 30 p | £ 60 | £ 30 |

| £ 20 | 20 p | 11 p | 7 p | £ 50 | £ 40 | 90 p |

6 In the park

5 Can I help you? Leseverstehen

Voraussetzungen
Schriftbild: Lebensmittel, Einkauf, Adjektive

S lesen die Texte. Sie erkennen die richtige Dialogfolge und nummerieren die Sätze entsprechend. Die nicht passenden Äußerungen werden durchgestrichen.

①
- [3] Here you are.
- [1] Can I help you?
- [ ] ~~I don't like carrots.~~
- [4] Thank you.
- [2] Yes, please. I'd like a sandwich.

②
- [ ] ~~I'm cold.~~
- [1] I'm hot.
- [3] Good idea. Cherry ice cream for me, please.
- [2] What about some ice cream?

③
- [5] Yes, I do.
- [1] I'm thirsty.
- [ ] ~~I'm hungry.~~
- [4] Oh, you don't like apple juice. Do you like orange juice?
- [2] I've got some apple juice for you.
- [3] No thank you.

6 What colour is it? Schreiben

Voraussetzungen
Schriftbild: Farben, Lebensmittel, Obst

S lesen die Wörter im Kasten. Sie ordnen die Lebensmittel den vorgegebenen Farben zu bzw. ergänzen die fehlenden Farben und schreiben die Wörter auf.
Einzelne Wörter (z. B. *apple*, *tea*) können auch mehrmals aufgeschrieben werden.

apple · banana · carrot · cherries · chocolate · ~~lemon~~ · lettuce · milk · ~~orange~~ · orange · peach · peanuts · strawberry · water · yellow

- brown: chocolate, peanuts,
- orange: orange, carrot, (peach)
- red: cherries, strawberry, (apple), (peach)
- yellow: lemon, banana, (apple)
- green: lettuce, (apple)
- white: milk
- no colour: water

Name _____ Date _____

5 Can I help you? Read the dialogues. Number the sentences.
Cross out the wrong sentences.

1
- [ ] Here you are.
- [ ] Can I help you?
- [ ] I don't like carrots.
- [ ] Thank you.
- [ ] Yes, please. I'd like a sandwich.

2
- [ ] I'm cold.
- [ ] I'm hot.
- [ ] Good idea. Cherry ice cream for me, please.
- [ ] What about some ice cream?

3
- [ ] Yes, I do.
- [ ] I'm thirsty.
- [ ] I'm hungry.
- [ ] Oh, you don't like apple juice. Do you like orange juice?
- [ ] I've got some apple juice for you.
- [ ] No thank you.

Name _____ Date _____

6 What colour is it? Write the words next to the right colour.
Some words can go with more than one colour.

| apple · banana · carrot · cherries · chocolate · ~~lemon~~ · lettuce · milk · ~~orange~~ · orange · peach · peanuts · strawberry · water · yellow |

brown: _____

_____ : orange,

red: _____

_____ : lemon,

green: _____

white: _____

no colour: _____

41

1 A trip to London

1 London sights Hörverstehen

Voraussetzungen
Sehenswürdigkeiten in London, Fahrzeuge, Uhrzeit, Preise

Spielen Sie die Dialoge von der CD.
S nummerieren die Sehenswürdigkeiten und verbinden sie mit den zutreffenden Informationen.
Ein weiteres Hören dient der Kontrolle.

CD track 25
Number 1
Girl: Let's go to Buckingham Palace.
Boy: Great. When?
Girl: On Sunday.
Boy: What time? At ten o'clock?
Girl: No, at eleven o'clock.
Boy: OK.

Number 2
Boy: How much is a ticket to London Zoo?
Busdriver: It's £1.70.
Boy: Two tickets please.
Busdriver: Here you are. That's £3.40.
Boy: Thank you.

Number 3
Girl 1: Let's go to Big Ben.
Girl 2: By underground?
Girl 1: No, let's go by bus.
Girl 2: What number is the bus to Big Ben?
Girl 1: It's number 60.
Girl 2: There's the bus.
Girl 1: No, that's bus number 40.

Number 4
Boy 1: What about going to Hyde Park?
Boy 2: No, let's go to Tower Bridge.
Boy 1: OK, good idea. Let's go by underground.
Boy 2: That's boring.
Boy 1: What about going by bus?
Boy 2: Let's go by boat. I like the River Thames.
Boy 1: OK then. Let's go.

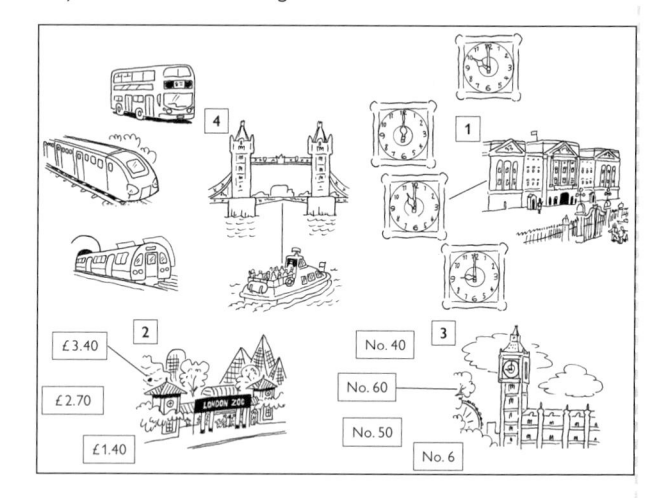

2 Where was Tom in the holidays? Hörverstehen; Leseverstehen

Voraussetzungen
Schriftbild: Ferien

S lesen die Sätze. Sie hören die Fragen nacheinander von der CD, finden die passenden Antworten und nummerieren diese entsprechend.
Ein weiteres Hören dient der Kontrolle.

CD track 26
Number 1: Where was Tom in the holidays?
Number 2: Do you speak German, Tom?
Number 3: Where were you in your holidays, Sally?
Number 4: Were you in Rome, Jenny?
Number 5: How were your holidays, Luke?
Number 6: Was it nice in London?

A trip to London 1

Name _____   Date _____

1 London sights Listen. Number the pictures. Draw lines.

track 25

£ 3.40

£ 2.70

£ 1.40

No. 40

No. 60

No. 50

No. 6

Name _____   Date _____

2 Where was Tom in the holidays? Read. Listen and number the right answers.

track 26

☐ I was at home.

☐ He was in Germany.

☐ Yes, it was super! I like the London Eye!

☐ No, I was in Ankara.

☐ Yes, I do. "Guten Morgen."

☐ OK.

43

1 A trip to London

3 What about going to Big Ben? Leseverstehen

Voraussetzungen
Schriftbild: Sehenswürdigkeiten in London, Fahrzeuge, Uhrzeit, Preise

S lesen die Texte.
Sie ergänzen die nummerierten Sätze in den Aufgaben, indem sie die richtigen Abbildungen abhaken.

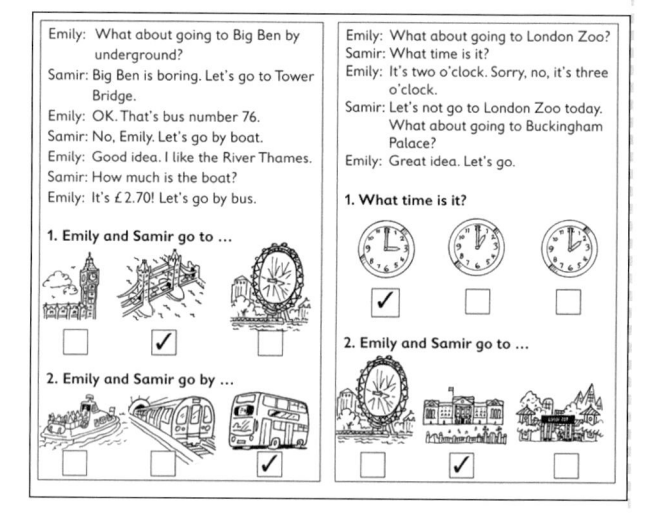

```
Emily:  What about going to Big Ben by
        underground?
Samir:  Big Ben is boring. Let's go to Tower
        Bridge.
Emily:  OK. That's bus number 76.
Samir:  No, Emily. Let's go by boat.
Emily:  Good idea. I like the River Thames.
Samir:  How much is the boat?
Emily:  It's £2.70! Let's go by bus.

1. Emily and Samir go to …
2. Emily and Samir go by …
```

```
Emily:  What about going to London Zoo?
Samir:  What time is it?
Emily:  It's two o'clock. Sorry, no, it's three
        o'clock.
Samir:  Let's not go to London Zoo today.
        What about going to Buckingham
        Palace?
Emily:  Great idea. Let's go.

1. What time is it?
2. Emily and Samir go to …
```

4 In London Leseverstehen

Voraussetzungen
Schriftbild: Fahrzeuge, Farben

S lesen die Sätze.
Sie überprüfen die Aussagen und malen die abgebildeten Fahrzeuge in den richtigen Farben an.

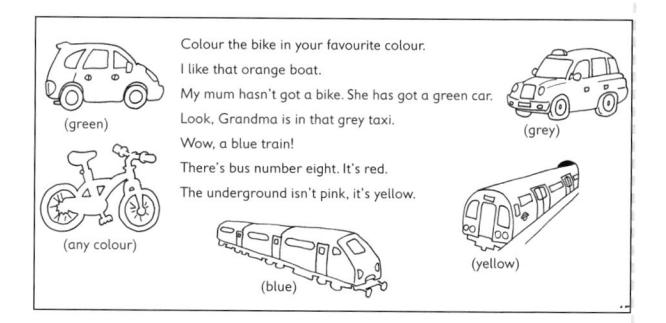

```
Colour the bike in your favourite colour.
I like that orange boat.
My mum hasn't got a bike. She has got a green car.
Look, Grandma is in that grey taxi.
Wow, a blue train!
There's bus number eight. It's red.
The underground isn't pink, it's yellow.

(green)    (grey)
(any colour)    (blue)    (yellow)
```

A trip to London 1

Name _____ Date _____

3 What about going to Big Ben? Read. Tick the right pictures.

Emily: What about going to Big Ben by underground?
Samir: Big Ben is boring. Let's go to Tower Bridge.
Emily: OK. That's bus number 76.
Samir: No, Emily. Let's go by boat.
Emily: Good idea. I like the River Thames.
Samir: How much is the boat?
Emily: It's £2.70! Let's go by bus.

1. Emily and Samir go to …

2. Emily and Samir go by …

Emily: What about going to London Zoo?
Samir: What time is it?
Emily: It's two o'clock. Sorry, no, it's three o'clock.
Samir: Let's not go to London Zoo today. What about going to Buckingham Palace?
Emily: Great idea. Let's go.

1. What time is it?

2. Emily and Samir go to …

Name _____ Date _____

4 In London Read the sentences. Colour the pictures.

Colour the bike in your favourite colour.

I like that orange boat.

My mum hasn't got a bike. She has got a green car.

Look, Grandma is in that grey taxi.

Wow, a blue train!

There's bus number eight. It's red.

The underground isn't pink, it's yellow.

1 A trip to London

5 Seven days Schreiben

Voraussetzungen
Schriftbild: Wochentage

S sehen sich die Kalendereintragungen an. Sie lesen die Wörter im Wortkasten und vervollständigen die Sätze.

```
Monday · Friday · Saturday · Sunday · Thursday · Tuesday · Wednesday ·
at a birthday party · at home · at my grandma's · in London · in the garden shed ·
in the park · with my friends
```

MON	TUE	WED	THU	FRI	SAT	SUN

I was at my grandma's on Monday.
I was in the garden shed on Tuesday.
I was with my friends on Wednesday.
I was in the park on Thursday.
I was in London on Friday.
I was at home on Saturday.
I was at a birthday party on Sunday.

6 A whale in the River Thames Leseverstehen; Schreiben

Voraussetzungen
Story: A whale in the River Thames

S lesen den Text. Sie wählen die jeweils zur Geschichte passenden Wörter und Satzteile im Wortkasten aus und vervollständigen den Text.

```
happy · whale · Friday · Saturday · Sunday · Thursday ·
Big Ben · London Eye · River Thames · Tower Bridge ·
What a big bridge! · What a big clock tower! · What a big wheel! · Where's my dad?
```

There was a whale in the River Thames.
Thursday: The whale was under Tower Bridge. 'Wow! What a big bridge!'
Friday: There was the London Eye. 'Wow! What a big wheel!'
Saturday: And there was Big Ben. 'Wow! What a big clock tower!'
But the whale wasn't happy. 'Where's my mum?
Where's my dad?'
'Bye-bye, Big Ben
Bye-bye, London Eye
Bye-bye Tower Bridge'.
Sunday: 'Hello, Mum. Hello, Dad.'
The whale was happy.

A trip to London   1

Name _____   Date _____

5 Seven days Read the words in the box. Write the sentences.

| ~~Monday~~ · Friday · Saturday · Sunday · Thursday · Tuesday · Wednesday · |
| at a birthday party · at home · ~~at my grandma's~~ · in London · in the garden shed · |
| in the park · with my friends |

| MON | TUE | WED | THU | FRI | SAT | SUN |

I was _at my grandma's_ on _Monday_. _____.

I was _____ on _____. _____.

I was _____ on _____. _____.

I _____. _____.

Name _____   Date _____

6 A whale in the River Thames Write the story.

| happy · whale · Friday · Saturday · Sunday · Thursday · |
| Big Ben · London Eye · River Thames · Tower Bridge · |
| What a big bridge! · What a big clock tower! · What a big wheel! · Where's my dad? |

There was a whale in the _____.

_____ : The whale was under Tower Bridge. 'Wow! _____,'

_____ : There was the London Eye. 'Wow! _____,'

_____ : And there was Big Ben. 'Wow! _____,'

But the whale wasn't _____. 'Where's my mum?

_____,

'Bye-bye, _____.

Bye-bye, _____.

Bye-bye _____,'

_____ : 'Hello, Mum. Hello, Dad.'

The _____ was happy.

2 All year round

1 What's the weather like in Rome? Hörverstehen

Voraussetzungen
Wetter, Zahlen 20–100

Spielen Sie den Hörtext mit den Wetterangaben vor. S hören zunächst nur zu.
Beim wiederholten Hören tragen sie die Wettersymbole bzw. die genannten Temperaturen in die Kästen ein.
Ein letztes Hören dient der Kontrolle.

CD track 27
Good morning. This is Radio Rome.
It's sunny today and it's windy.

Hi Mum. Yes. I'm in Berlin.
The weather? Well, it isn't rainy today, but it's cloudy and foggy.

Today's weather in Ankara:
It's cloudy, but it's hot – thirty degrees.

Dear Grandma. It's so cold here in London.
The temperature is two degrees and it's snowy.

What's the weather like in New York?
Twenty degrees and rainy. It's a warm day.

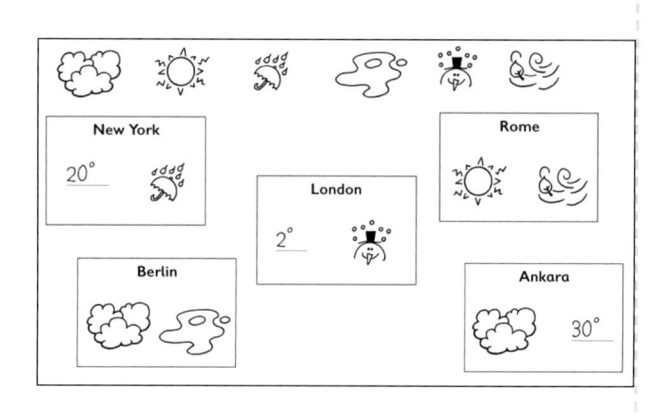

2 Bingo Hörverstehen

Voraussetzungen
Zahlen 13–19, 21 ff.

Spielen Sie den Hörtext abschnittweise vor.
S streichen die Zahlen aus, die genannt werden. Wenn sie vier Zahlen angekreuzt haben, die sich in einer Linie befinden, heben sie die Hand und rufen „Bingo!".
Zur Kontrolle wird der CD-Text noch einmal gehört.

CD track 28
Number 1
7 – 11 – 8 – 15 – 13 – 70 – 40

Number 2
21 – 31 – 12 – 28 – 80 – 20 – 30

All year round 2

Name _____   Date _____

1 What's the weather like in Rome?
Listen. Draw the weather symbols. Write the temperature.

New York		Rome
	London	
Berlin		Ankara

Name _____   Date _____

2 Bingo Listen. Cross out the numbers. Say 'Bingo!'

①

BINGO			
2	14	10	40
29	12	7	16
50	8	70	15
13	3	11	6

②

BINGO			
31	24	29	19
32	80	25	23
20	28	12	30
22	21	17	13

2 All year round

3 Seasons and months Leseverstehen; Schreiben

Voraussetzungen
Schriftbild: Monate, Jahreszeiten

S lesen die Sätze und unterstreichen jeweils den Monat, der in die vorgegebene Jahreszeit fällt. Sie vervollständigen die Verbindung der Monate in der richtigen Reihenfolge und ergänzen die fehlenden Monatsnamen.

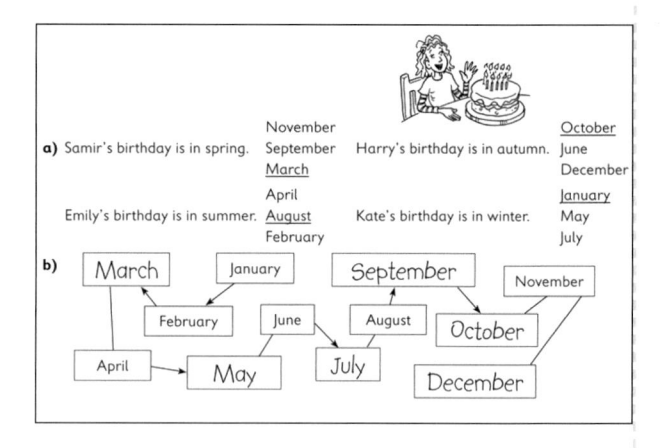

4 What a nice day Leseverstehen

Voraussetzungen
Schriftbild: Wetter, Lebensmittel, Haustiere, Verkehrsmittel

S sehen sich die Abbildungen an. Sie lesen die darunterstehenden Texte und kreisen die zutreffenden Wörter ein.
Sie lesen die unten aufgeführten Wörter und nummerieren die Gegenstände in den Bildern entsprechend.

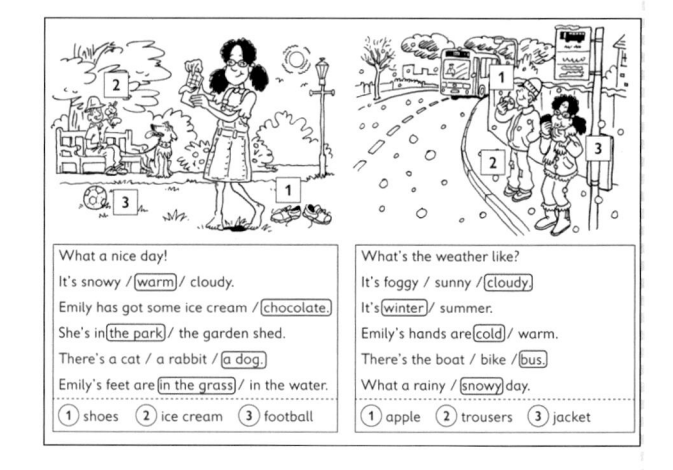

All year round 2

Name _____ Date _____

3 Seasons and months

a) Underline the right month.

b) Write the missing words. Draw the missing lines.

a) Samir's birthday is in spring.
November
September
March

Harry's birthday is in autumn.
October
June
December

Emily's birthday is in summer.
April
August
February

Kate's birthday is in winter.
January
May
July

b)

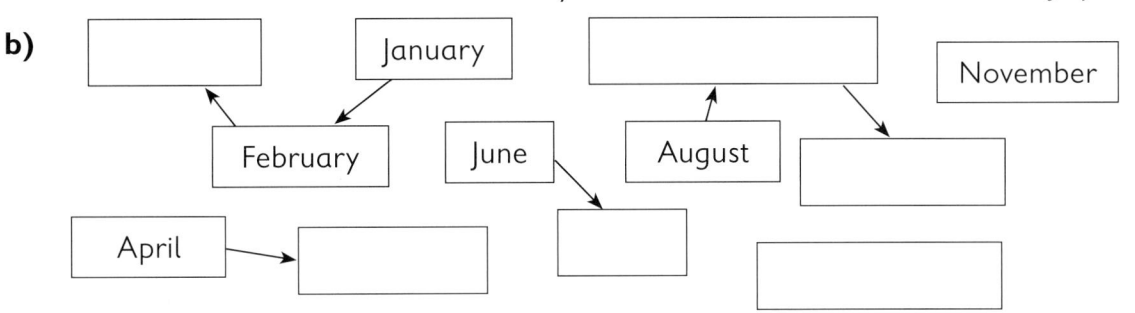

☐	← January	☐	November
February	June →	August → ☐	
April → ☐			☐

Name _____ Date _____

4 What a nice day Look at the pictures. Read the texts. Circle the correct words. Read the words. Write the numbers.

What a nice day!	What's the weather like?
It's snowy / warm / cloudy.	It's foggy / sunny / cloudy.
Emily has got some ice cream / chocolate.	It's winter / summer.
She's in the park / the garden shed.	Emily's hands are cold / warm.
There's a cat / a rabbit / a dog.	There's the boat / bike / bus.
Emily's feet are in the grass / in the water.	What a rainy / snowy day.
① shoes ② ice cream ③ football	① apple ② trousers ③ jacket

51

2 All year round

5 Today is Sunday Schreiben

Voraussetzungen
Schriftbild: Wetter, Wochentage

S lesen die Wörter. Sie sehen sich die Wettersymbole im Kalender an und schreiben auf, wie das Wetter an den jeweiligen Wochentagen war. Anschließend schreiben sie ihren eigenen Wetterbericht.

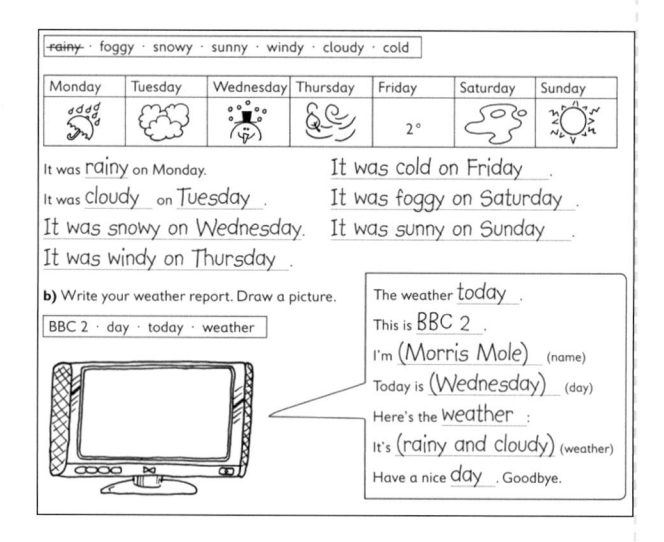

6 Roses in summer Schreiben

Voraussetzungen
Schriftbild: Wetter, Jahreszeiten, Natur

S lesen die Wörter und beschriften die Abbildungen.

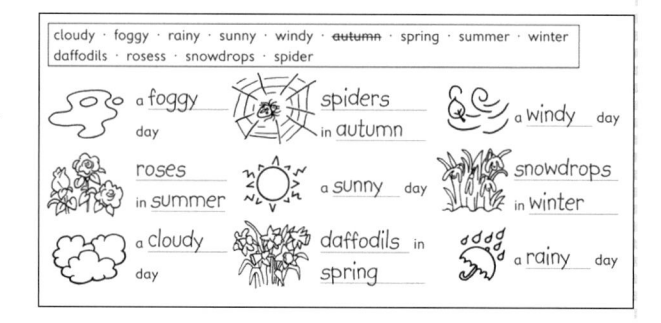

52

All year round 2

Name _____ Date _____

5 Today is Sunday a) Read the words. Write the sentences.

| ~~rainy~~ · foggy · snowy · sunny · windy · cloudy · cold |

Monday	Tuesday	Wednesday	Thursday	Friday	Saturday	Sunday
				2°		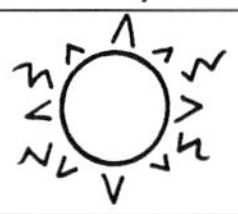

It was rainy on Monday.   _____.

It was _____ on _____.   _____.

_____.   _____.

_____.

b) Write your weather report. Draw a picture.

| BBC 2 · day · today · weather |

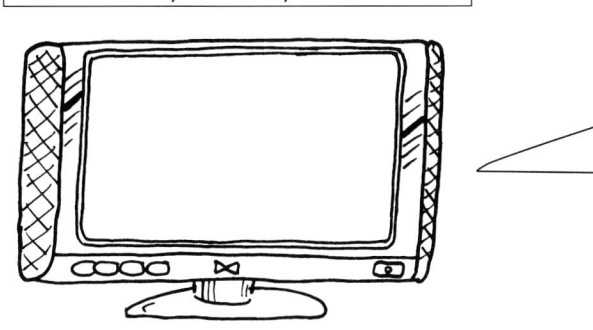

The weather _____.

This is _____.

I'm _____ (name)

Today is _____ (day)

Here's the _____:

It's _____ (weather)

Have a nice _____. Goodbye.

Name _____ Date _____

6 Roses in summer Read. Write the words. You can colour the pictures.

| cloudy · foggy · rainy · sunny · windy · ~~autumn~~ · spring · summer · winter
daffodils · rosess · snowdrops · spider |

a _____ day

_____ in autumn

a _____ day

_____ in _____

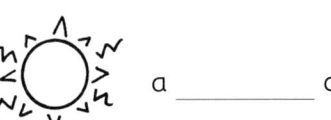

a _____ day

_____ in _____

a _____ day

_____ in _____

a _____ day

53

3 At the museum

1 Where are the monkeys? Hörverstehen

Voraussetzungen
Tiere, Adverbien, Zahlen 13–100

Spielen Sie die Dialoge von der CD.
S entscheiden anhand der Angaben, ob man treppauf oder treppab gehen muss, und markieren dies durch Pfeile.
Beim erneuten Hören tragen sie ein, in welchen Räumen sich die genannten Tiere befinden.
Zur Kontrolle wird der CD-Text erneut vorgespielt.

CD track 29
Girl: Excuse me, please. Where are the monkeys?
Man: They're upstairs, in room 27.

Boy: Excuse me, please. Where's the whale?
Woman: It's downstairs, in room 54.

Girl: Excuse me, please. Where are the lions?
Woman: They're downstairs, in room 35.

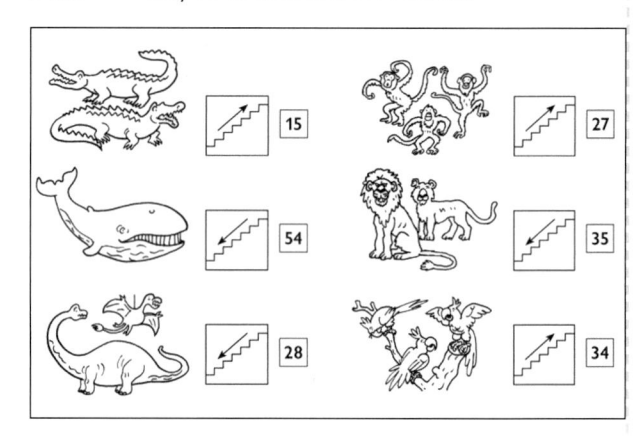

Boy: Excuse me, please. Where are the parrots?
Man: They're upstairs, in room 34.

Boy: Excuse me, please. Where are the crocodiles?
Woman: They're upstairs, in room 15.

Girl: Excuse me, please. Where are the dinosaurs?
Man: They're downstairs, in room 28.

2 Which animal is it? Hörverstehen; Schreiben

Voraussetzungen
Körperteile, Natur, Adjektive;
Schriftbild: Tiere

Spielen Sie den Hörtext von der CD.
S finden heraus, welche Tiere beschrieben werden, und nummerieren die Abbildungen entsprechend.
Zur Kontrolle wird der Hörtext erneut abgespielt.
Anschließend schreiben S die Namen der Tiere, die sie erkannt haben.

CD track 30
Number 1
(Peep) live in the jungle.
They've got long arms and legs.
You can see (Peep) in a zoo.
They are funny.

Number 2
(Peep) have got strong teeth.
They live in the bush.
They eat small animals and big animals.

Number 3
(Peep) live in the garden.
They are wild animals but they are small.
(Peep) are black.
They've got a long nose and a short tail.

Number 4
(Peep) live in trees.
They can be red or green or yellow or blue.
Some children have got a (Peep) as a pet.
They are loud and they can talk.

Number 5
(Peep) like grass and trees. They are grey.
They've got big ears and a long nose.
(Peep) are strong animals.

Number 1: monkey
Number 2: lion
Number 3: mole
Number 4: parrot
Number 5: elephant

At the museum 3

Name _____ Date _____

1 Where are the monkeys? Listen. Draw: upstairs [↗] downstairs [↘].
Write the room numbers.

track 29

Name _____ Date _____

2 Which animal is it? Listen. Number the pictures. Write the names of the animals.

track 30

| elephant · dinosaur · mole · lion · monkey · whale · crocodile · parrot · rabbit |

Number 1: _____
Number 2: _____
Number 3: _____
Number 4: _____
Number 5: _____

3 At the museum

3 They've got big ears Leseverstehen

Voraussetzungen
Schriftbild: Körperteile, Natur, Adjektive

S lesen die Beschreibungen der Fantasietiere und verbinden die Sätze mit den passenden Abbildungen.

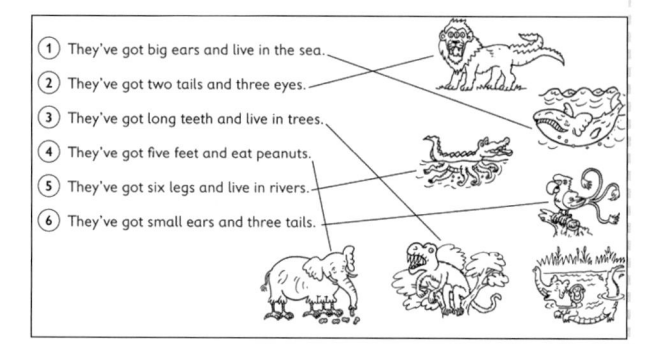

1. They've got big ears and live in the sea.
2. They've got two tails and three eyes.
3. They've got long teeth and live in trees.
4. They've got five feet and eat peanuts.
5. They've got six legs and live in rivers.
6. They've got small ears and three tails.

4 Whales live in the sea Leseverstehen; Schreiben

Voraussetzungen
Schriftbild: Tiere, Natur, Adjektive

S lesen die Wörter und Satzteile im Wortkasten. Sie sehen sich die Abbildungen an und vervollständigen die Sätze.

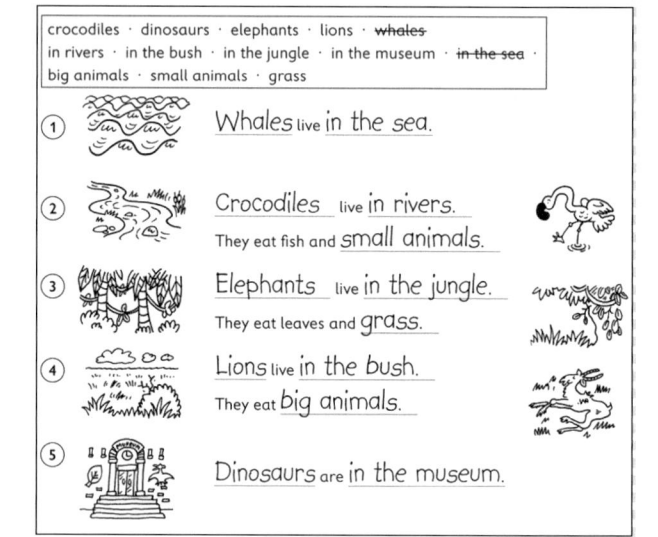

crocodiles · dinosaurs · elephants · lions · ~~whales~~
in rivers · in the bush · in the jungle · in the museum · ~~in the sea~~
big animals · small animals · grass

1. Whales live in the sea.
2. Crocodiles live in rivers. They eat fish and small animals.
3. Elephants live in the jungle. They eat leaves and grass.
4. Lions live in the bush. They eat big animals.
5. Dinosaurs are in the museum.

At the museum 3

Name _____   Date _____

3 They've got big ears Read the sentences. Draw lines.

1. They've got big ears and live in the sea.
2. They've got two tails and three eyes.
3. They've got long teeth and live in trees.
4. They've got five feet and eat peanuts.
5. They've got six legs and live in rivers.
6. They've got small ears and three tails.

Name _____   Date _____

4 Whales live in the sea Read the words. Write the sentences.

| crocodiles · dinosaurs · elephants · lions · ~~whales~~ |
| in rivers · in the bush · in the jungle · in the museum · ~~in the sea~~ |
| big animals · small animals · grass |

1. Whales live in the sea.

2. _____ live _____.
   They eat fish and _____.

3. _____ live _____.
   They eat leaves and _____.

4. _____ live _____.
   They eat _____.

5. _____ are _____.

57

3 At the museum

5 I wish I had an elephant's big ears Schreiben

Voraussetzungen
Schriftbild: Körperteile, Adjektive;
Story: Harry's night at the museum

S lesen die Wörter im Wortkasten. Sie beschriften die Abbildung und vervollständigen den Text.

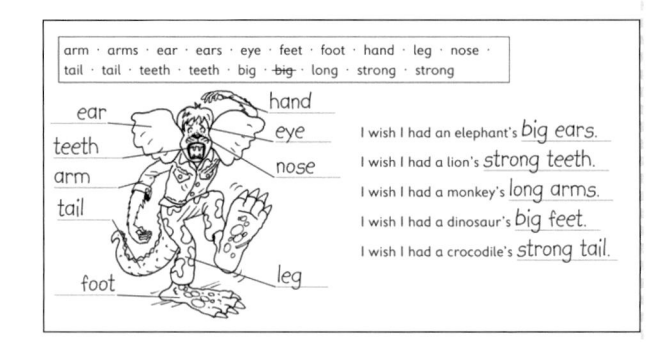

6 I want to speak about ... Leseverstehen; Schreiben

Voraussetzungen
Schriftbild: Tiere, Körperteile, Natur, Adjektive

S lesen den Text. Sie haken die sechs Aussagen ab, die zu dem Tier passen, über das Emily spricht.
Sie vervollständigen die Sprechblase mit dem Namen des entsprechenden Tieres.
S schreiben Emilys Vortrag im Ganzen ab.

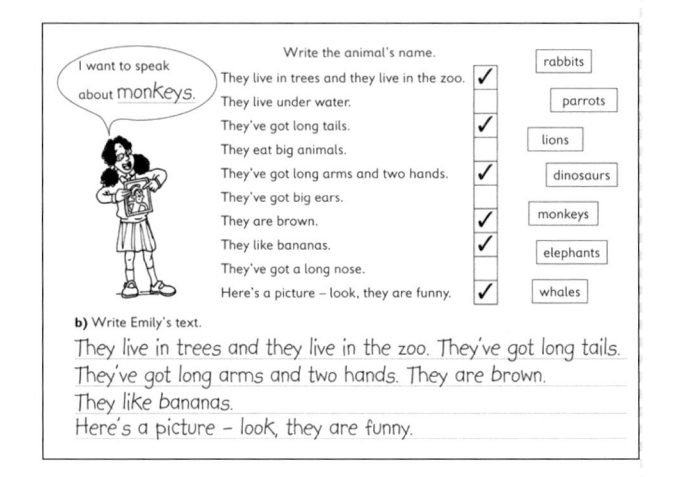

At the museum 3

Name _____ Date _____

5 I wish I had an elephant's big ears Read and write the words.
Complete the sentences.

arm · arms · ear · ears · eye · feet · foot · hand · leg · nose · tail · tail · teeth · teeth · big · ~~big~~ · long · strong · strong

I wish I had an elephant's *big* _____

I wish I had a lion's _____

I wish I had a monkey's _____

I wish I had a dinosaur's _____

I wish I had a crocodile's _____

Name _____ Date _____

6 I want to speak about … a) Read and tick Emily's 6 sentences.
Write the animal's name.

I want to speak about _____

They live in trees and they live in the zoo.
They live under water.
They've got long tails.
They eat big animals.
They've got long arms and two hands.
They've got big ears.
They are brown.
They like bananas.
They've got a long nose.
Here's a picture – look, they are funny.

rabbits
parrots
lions
dinosaurs
monkeys
elephants
whales

b) Write Emily's text.

_____
_____
_____
_____

59

4 Keeping fit

1 Stretch your arms Hörverstehen

Voraussetzungen
Körperteile, Bewegungen

Spielen Sie den Hörtext von der CD.
S ordnen die Anweisungen den entsprechenden
Abbildungen zu und nummerieren diese.
Ein weiteres Abspielen des Hörtextes dient der
Kontrolle.

CD track 31
Number 1:   Stretch your arms.
Number 2:   Touch your knees.
Number 3:   Put your head on the chair.
Number 4:   Hop to the window.
Number 5:   Bend your arms.
Number 6:   Touch your shoulders.
Number 7:   Put your right leg under the table.
Number 8:   Hop to the door.
Number 9:   Put your left leg under the table.
Number 10: Hop to the board.

2 I can't dance Hörverstehen

Voraussetzungen
Sportarten

S hören die Aussagen von der CD.
Je nachdem, ob die Kinder eine Sportart
beherrschen oder nicht, zeichnen S ein „Smiley"
oder ein „Frowney" in die Tabelle ein.
Zur Kontrolle wird der CD-Text noch einmal
gehört.

CD track 32
Hi, I'm Mark. I can't dance but I can play football
and table tennis.

Hi, I'm Jackie. I can ride a horse and I can swim,
but I can't ski.

Hi, I'm Susan. I can do judo. Judo is great. I can't ride a
horse and I can't play football.

Hi, I'm Chris. I like water and I can swim.
I like music but I can't dance.

Keeping fit 4

Name _____ Date _____

1 Stretch your arms Listen. Number the pictures.

track 31

Name _____ Date _____

2 I can't dance Listen. What can or can't they do? Draw the faces: 🙂 ☹ .

track 32

Jackie							
Mark							
Susan							
Chris							

4 Keeping fit

3 Go to the door Hörverstehen; Leseverstehen; Schreiben

Voraussetzungen
Schriftbild: Körperteile, Bewegungen

Spielen Sie den Hörtext von der CD.
S verbinden die „Übungsorte" in der gehörten Reihenfolge mit Linien.
Sie hören den Text ein weiteres Mal und nummerieren die Aktivitäten.
Sie schreiben auf, was an der jeweiligen Station getan werden soll. Zur Kontrolle wird der CD-Text abschließend noch einmal gehört.

CD track 33
Number 1: Go to the door. Stretch your arms.
Number 2: Go to a table. Put your foot on the table and touch your toes.
Number 3: Go to the window. Oh, it's sunny today. You are happy and you hop on your right leg.
Number 4: Go to the board. Touch your shoulders.
Number 5: Go to your chair. Bend and put your head on the chair.

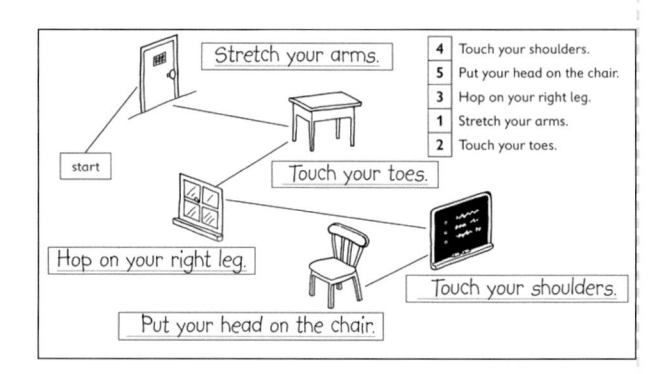

4 Draw a monster Leseverstehen

Voraussetzungen
Schriftbild: Körperteile, Adjektive, Farben

S lesen zunächst die vollständige Beschreibung. Anschließend zeichnen sie schrittweise das Monster auf dem Skateboard und malen die Körperteile in den angegebenen Farben aus.

Keeping fit 4

Name _____ Date _____

3 Go to the door Listen. Draw lines from station to station. Number the activities. Write the activities.

track 33

☐ Touch your shoulders.
☐ Put your head on the chair.
☐ Hop on your right leg.
☐ Stretch your arms.
☐ Touch your toes.

start

Name _____ Date _____

4 Draw a monster Read the sentences. Draw the monster. Colour it.

1. What a big monster! It has got a big head.
2. Draw two small orange ears.
3. It has got three eyes. They're yellow.
4. It has got a short red nose.
5. It has got five long teeth. They're blue.
6. There's a mole on the monster's shoulder.
7. The monster has got three arms.
8. It has got one leg. The foot has got two toes.
9. The monster has got a pink tail.
10. The monster is on a green skateboard.

My monster

4 Keeping fit

5 I can ride a horse Leseverstehen, Schreiben

Voraussetzungen
Schriftbild: Sportarten

S sehen sich die Abbildungen an. Sie wählen die passenden Wörter aus und schreiben auf, welche Sportarten die Kinder beherrschen bzw. nicht beherrschen.

```
ride a horse · play table tennis · play computer games ·
dance · do judo · ski · swim · go by bike · listen to music
```

👍 I can ride a horse.
👎 I can't swim.
👎 I can't dance.
👍 I can play table tennis.
👎 I can't do judo.
👍 I can ski.

6 Emily, the sports star Leseverstehen; Schreiben

Voraussetzungen
Story: Emily, the sports star

S lesen die Wörter und Satzteile im Wortkasten und vervollständigen den Lückentext.

```
bedroom · dance · Fit kids club · garden · great · hop · house · I can't stretch ·
knees · o'clock · play · read a book · She isn't · the sports star
```

Emily, the sports star.
Samir, Kate and Harry want to go to the Fit kids club.
Emily: I can't go. I've got to read a book.
Samir: No, no! No excuses!
It's 4 o'clock. The friends are at Emily's house. Where's Emily?
She isn't playing a computer game in the bedroom.
She isn't in the bathroom. Emily is in the garden.
Emily: Ouch, I can't bend my knees. I can't stretch my arms.
Harry: Come, Emily. Let's go to the fitness class.
In the Fit kids club the children hop and play and dance.
Emily: Oh, I like it. The Fit kids club is great.

Keeping fit 4

Name _____ Date _____

5 I can ride a horse Write what the children can do 👍 and can't do 👎.

ride a horse · play table tennis · play computer games ·
dance · do judo · ski · swim · go by bike · listen to music

👍 I can _____ .

👎 I can't _____ .

👎 _____ .

👍 _____ .

👎 _____ .

👍 _____ .

Name _____ Date _____

6 Emily, the sports star Read the story. Fill in the missing words.

bedroom · dance · Fit kids club · garden · great · hop · house · I can't stretch ·
knees · o'clock · play · read a book · She isn't · the sports star

Emily, _____ .

Samir, Kate and Harry want to go to the _____ .

Emily: I can't go. I've got to _____ .

Samir: No, no! No excuses!

It's 4 _____ The friends are at Emily's _____ . Where's Emily?

She isn't playing a computer game in the _____ .

_____ in the bathroom. Emily is in the _____ .

Emily: Ouch, I can't bend my _____ . _____ my arms.

Harry: Come, Emily. Let's go to the fitness class.

In the Fit kids club the children _____ and _____ and _____ .

Emily: Oh, I like it. The Fit kids club is _____ .

5 Emails from the USA

1 Thanks for your email Hörverstehen

Voraussetzungen
Haustiere, Monate, Hobbys, Familie, Berufe

Spielen Sie den Hörtext von der CD.
S betrachten die Abbildungen, wählen die jeweils passende aus und haken sie ab.
Ein weiteres Abspielen des Hörtextes dient der Kontrolle.

CD track 34
Number 1
Hi, Tom. Thanks for your email. I'm nine years old.
Number 2
My birthday is in May.
Number 3
I've got a brother. He's three years old.
Number 4
My mother is a shop assistant and my father is a mechanic.
Number 5
My hobbies are playing table tennis and playing computer games.
Number 6
I like my pets. I've got a guinea pig and a rabbit. Have you got any pets? Your friend Paul.

2 I was in New York in summer Leseverstehen; Schreiben

Voraussetzungen
Schriftbild: Sehenswürdigkeiten in New York, Wetter, Verkehrsmittel, Hobbys, Berufe

S lesen den Text und kreisen diejenigen Wörter ein, die nicht in den Zusammenhang passen.
Weisen Sie S darauf hin, dass in den meisten Sätzen ein Wort falsch bzw. überzählig ist. Einige Sätze enthalten jedoch auch zwei bzw. gar keine Fehler.
S schreiben die Lösungssätze auf, die sich aus den Wörtern ergeben, und malen ein passendes Bild dazu.

I was in New York in ⌐I've¬ summer. It was hot.
New York ⌐got¬ is a great ⌐a¬ city.
There are ⌐friend¬ skyscrapers.
The taxis are ⌐He¬ yellow.
I wish I was a taxi ⌐has¬ driver in ⌐got¬ New York.
I was at the Statue of Liberty.
And I was ⌐a¬ playing ⌐skateboard¬ football in Central Park.

I've got a friend .
He has got a skateboard .

Please draw:

Emails from the USA 5

Name _____   Date _____

1 Thanks for your email Listen. Tick the right pictures.

2 I was in New York in summer
a) Read the text. Which words don't fit?
b) Circle the words and write the sentences.
c) Draw a picture.

I was in New York in I've summer. It was hot.

New York got is a great ⓐ city.

There are friend skyscrapers.

The taxis are He yellow.

I wish I was a taxi has driver in got New York.

I was at the Statue of Liberty.

And I was a playing skateboard football in Central Park.

Please draw:

67

5 Emails from the USA

3 I want an e-pal Leseverstehen

Voraussetzungen
Schriftbild: Fragen und Antworten der Units 1–5 (Band 2)

S lesen die Fragen und haken die richtigen Antworten ab.

① What's your mother's job?
☐ He's a bus driver. ✓ She's a taxi driver.
② Have you got a pet?
✓ Yes, I have. ☐ Yes, I do.
③ When's your birthday?
☐ In the park. ✓ In summer.
④ How old is your brother?
☐ He is big. ✓ He is 4. ☐ She is 12.
⑤ Where's your e-pal from?
✓ She's from London. ☐ He has got a grandmother in London.
⑥ What's your hobby?
☐ I don't like swimming. ☐ My favourite pet is a hamster. ✓ I like doing judo.

4 Jobs Leseverstehen; Schreiben

Voraussetzungen
Schriftbild: Berufe

S lesen die Wörter. Sie vervollständigen die Sätze und verbinden diese mit den passenden Abbildungen auf der rechten Seite.

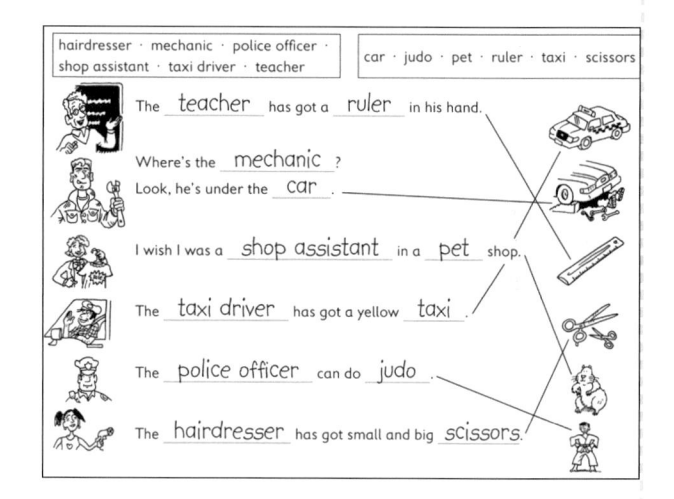

hairdresser · mechanic · police officer · shop assistant · taxi driver · teacher

car · judo · pet · ruler · taxi · scissors

The _teacher_ has got a _ruler_ in his hand.
Where's the _mechanic_ ? Look, he's under the _car_ .
I wish I was a _shop assistant_ in a _pet_ shop.
The _taxi driver_ has got a yellow _taxi_ .
The _police officer_ can do _judo_ .
The _hairdresser_ has got small and big _scissors_.

Emails from the USA 5

Name _____ Date _____

3 I want an e-pal Read the questions. Tick the right answers.

1) What's your mother's job?
   ☐ He's a bus driver.   ☐ She's a taxi driver.

2) Have you got a pet?
   ☐ Yes, I have.   ☐ Yes, I do.

3) When's your birthday?
   ☐ In the park.   ☐ In summer.

4) How old is your brother?
   ☐ He is big.   ☐ He is 4.   ☐ She is 12.

5) Where's your e-pal from?
   ☐ She's from London.   ☐ He has got a grandmother in London.

6) What's your hobby?
   ☐ I don't like swimming.   ☐ My favourite pet is a hamster.   ☐ I like doing judo.

Name _____ Date _____

4 Jobs Read. Fill in the missing words. Draw lines from the sentences to the pictures.

| hairdresser · mechanic · police officer · shop assistant · taxi driver · teacher | car · judo · pet · ruler · scissors · taxi |

The _____ has got a _____ in his hand.

Where's the _____?
Look, he's under the _____.

I wish I was a _____ in a _____ shop.

The _____ has got a yellow _____.

The _____ can do _____.

The _____ has got small and big _____.

5 Emails from the USA

5 A family tree Leseverstehen, Schreiben

Voraussetzungen
Schriftbild: Familie, Berufe

S lesen die Wörter im Wortkasten und ergänzen sie im Stammbaum und im Lückentext.

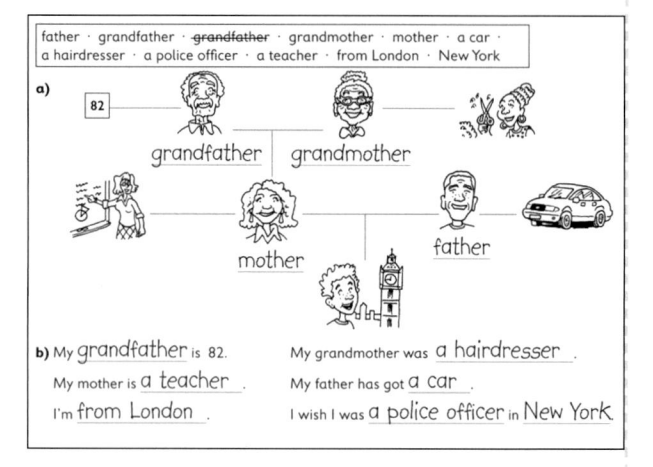

```
father · grandfather · grandfather · grandmother · mother · a car ·
a hairdresser · a police officer · a teacher · from London · New York
```

a) 82
grandfather   grandmother
mother   father

b) My grandfather is 82. My grandmother was a hairdresser.
My mother is a teacher. My father has got a car.
I'm from London. I wish I was a police officer in New York.

6 It's Brooklyn Bridge Leseverstehen; Schreiben

Voraussetzungen
Schriftbild: Sehenswürdigkeiten in New York

S verbinden die Abbildungen mit den Namen der Sehenswürdigkeiten.
Sie lesen die Sätze im Wortkasten, ordnen sie den Sehenswürdigkeiten zu und schreiben sie entsprechend auf.

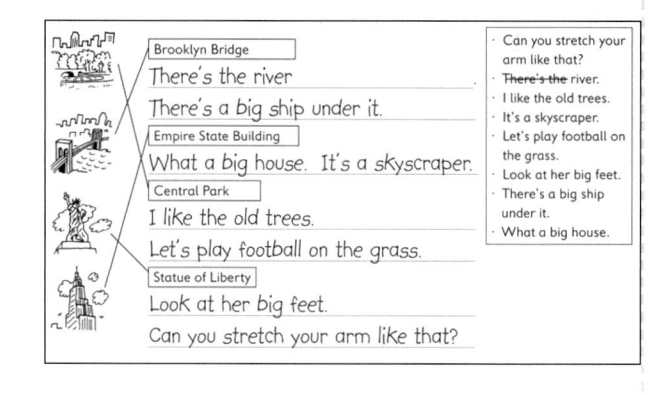

Brooklyn Bridge
There's the river.
There's a big ship under it.

Empire State Building
What a big house. It's a skyscraper.

Central Park
I like the old trees.
Let's play football on the grass.

Statue of Liberty
Look at her big feet.
Can you stretch your arm like that?

- Can you stretch your arm like that?
- There's the river.
- I like the old trees.
- It's a skyscraper.
- Let's play football on the grass.
- Look at her big feet.
- There's a big ship under it.
- What a big house.

Emails from the USA   5

Name _____   Date _____

5 A family tree a) Read. Write words under the pictures. **b)** Complete the sentences.

father · grandfather · ~~grandfather~~ · grandmother · mother · a car ·
a hairdresser · a police officer · a teacher · from London · New York

a)   82

grandfather

b) My _____ is 82.   My grandmother was _____.

My mother is _____.   My father has got _____.

I'm _____.   I wish I was _____ in _____.

Name _____   Date _____

6 It's Brooklyn Bridge Draw lines from the pictures to the names of the sights.
Read and write the sentences.

Brooklyn Bridge

There's the _____.

Empire State Building

_____

Central Park

_____

Statue of Liberty

_____

- Can you stretch your arm like that?
- ~~There's the~~ river.
- I like the old trees.
- It's a skyscraper.
- Let's play football on the grass.
- Look at her big feet.
- There's a big ship under it.
- What a big house.

Inhalt · Laufzeit 39:15

Track	Titel	Einzellaufzeit
1	Copyright	0:42

Band 1

Unit 1: Meeting friends

2	Exercise 1: That's English!	0:34
3	Exercise 2: What's the right number?	1:10
4	Exercise 3: What are they saying?	1:10

Unit 2: Pets in the garden

5	Exercise 1: There's a white T-shirt	0:50
6	Exercise 2: I've got a pet	0:54
7	Exercise 3: Food for the pets	1:02
8	Exercise 4: I like carrots	1:36

Unit 3: At school

9	Exercise 1: There's the school bus	1:38
10	Exercise 2: What's in your pencil case?	1:38
11	Exercise 3: School activities	0:44
12	Exercise 4: That's my rubber	0:45

Unit 4: The second-hand shop

13	Exercise 1: Clothes	0:41
14	Exercise 2: Too big or too small?	1:16
15	Exercise 3: Do you like the shoes?	1:06
16	Exercise 4: My hands are cold	0:51

Unit 5: Free-time activities

17	Exercise 1: I like reading	0:44
18	Exercise 2: A TV in Kate's bedroom	1:48
19	Exercise 3: Where's my school bag?	0:56
20	Exercise 4: Free-time activities	1:58

Unit 6: In the park

21	Exercise 1: I'm thirsty	0:56
22	Exercise 2: Shopping	1:05
23	Exercise 3: I like banana ice cream	1:10
24	Exercise 4: How much is the skateboard?	1:31

Band 2

Unit 1: A trip to London

25	Exercise 1: London sights	1:31
26	Exercise 2: Where was Tom in the holidays?	0:56

Unit 2: All year round

27	Exercise 1: What's the weather like in Rome?	1:07
28	Exercise 2: Bingo	1:11

Unit 3: At the museum

29	Exercise 1: Where are the monkeys?	1:21
30	Exercise 2: Which animal is it?	1:46

Unit 4: Keeping fit

31	Exercise 1: Stretch your arms	1:29
32	Exercise 2: I can't dance	0:52
33	Exercise 3: Go to the door	1:09

Unit 5: Emails from the USA

34	Exercise 1: Thanks for your email	1:07